Unleash Your Undeniable Impact

A compilation of messages to inspire you to maximize your impact in the world.

PRESENTED BY

LES BROWN AND DR. CHERYL WOOD

Publication Layout & Design: Literary Bae
www.literarybae.com

Contents

Foreword by
Les Brown

You have something special, you have GREATNESS in YOU!

If you have followed my career or heard me speak, then you know that I believe that all of us were born with a purpose and that we all have great gifts inside just waiting to be unleashed and shared with the world.

As much as I know this to be true, I can't tell you how many people I've met or who send me messages asking me to help them tap into or discover their purpose and the impact they're meant to make.

These people are a lot like I was many years ago, they are suffering from what I call, possibility blindness. They can't see the possibilities, potential, and promise that life holds for them. I understand how that feels. They feel like it's possible for others, but feel that they either aren't worthy or don't have what it takes to impact lives, walk into their purpose, and create a legacy.

Have you ever felt this way? I did for quite a long time, until I finally discovered that there is an UNDENIABLE IMPACT connected to my very being!

Guess what... You have UNDENIABLE IMPACT connected to your very being too!

I am excited to share with you Dr. Cheryl Wood's latest groundbreaking book, Unleash Your Undeniable Impact.

We all need a little coaching from time to time to help us walk into and/ or remain focused on the undeniable impact we're meant to make in the world and I'm glad that Cheryl is here to provide us with this gem. Prepare to uncover and overcome the mental and emotional barriers in your life that are blocking you from unleashing your undeniable impact and experiencing the fulfillment you can receive by sharing your gifts.

Dr. Wood shares with us that no matter what seems to be broken, imperfect, or flawed in you, that you can still have greatness in you and you can create great impact with your unique DNA. Now is the time for you to unleash what is inside of you!

There is no one in this world quite like you and we need what you have to offer.

I hope you're ready to transform your mind and your life, because reading these pages will certainly push you forward and accelerate your journey into greatness, purpose and impact.

I keep this book close by me to feel inspired and motivated. I'm sure you will too!

Remember, you have a unique fingerprint that no one can duplicate and no one can create the impact that can only be felt when you unleash what's inside of you!

That's my story and I'm sticking to it.

Les Brown
Speaker, Author, Trainer

Introduction by
Dr. Cheryl Wood

Compilation Visionary of Unleash Your Undeniable Impact
14x Best-Selling Author | International Empowerment Speaker |
TEDx Speaker | Speaker Development Coach | Leadership Expert

Without question, your unique impact on the world is undeniable! You are a force to be reckoned with! Your fingerprint is meant to touch lives globally! I need you to know that you are an irreplaceable expression of life, a one-of-a-kind precious masterpiece with intended impact that cannot be denied, the likes of which no one will ever see again. You are powerful beyond all measure. And you have everything you need to win big and achieve great things in your life. In fact, winning is in your DNA! You were created from greatness to manifest greatness. But, to manifest everything connected to your distinct greatness and to unleash your impact in the world, you must first believe that you are capable of accomplishing everything you set your mind to. You must develop a mindset of determination and a spirit of tenacity to press through anything that hinders you from becoming the greatest version of yourself.

From this moment forward, even in the face of any fears, doubts or self-limiting beliefs you may be holding onto, I challenge you to boldly embrace that you are fearfully and wonderfully made and that you have a divine calling on your life that is bigger than you! The calling on your life is connected to the countless people who are waiting to be impacted and inspired by you, those who will watch your journey and begin to unleash their impact and their gifts because you unleashed yours. Your example of unleashing your impact will shift the trajectory of countless lives around the world!

In this book, you will be reminded that unleashing your impact and living up to your fullest potential will require consistent courage, tenacity, drive, ambition, determination and commitment. On your journey, you will face challenges, obstacles, roadblocks and setbacks but your internal strength will equip you to bounce back from anything standing in the way of your destiny. Remind yourself daily of who you are and 'whose you are'!

As you immerse yourself into the powerful messages contained in this book, it is my hope that you will reignite the fire inside you to use your unique fingerprint to create a life you're in love with and to make a difference in the lives of others who will be inspired by your life journey. It is my hope that you will refuse to keep your greatness tucked on the inside but, rather, you will unleash everything God has given you as a gift to share with others.

In my own life, I had to go on a personal journey of discovering that I had greatness inside of me waiting to be unleashed even in spite of my past. As a young girl who was raised in poverty in an inner-city housing project in Baltimore, Maryland, I assumed that my life would be dictated by my environment. I assumed that people would judge who I could be based on where I had come from, and that I would just be another statistic. I didn't think I could ever make massive impact on the lives of others by sharing my God-given gifts. But there was a turning point when I started to shift my mindset and my perspective in order to make a decision that I didn't want to be a statistic. I wanted to rise above my past and become a change agent in the world. Once I made the decision to unleash my undeniable impact and walk fully in my divine purpose, there was a ripple effect that took place – my life started to change, my family's life started to change, and the lives of those I encountered through my work of empowerment started to change. And you have the same potential!

As you take a deep dive into the messages shared in Unleash Your Undeniable Impact, you will feel enlightened, reenergized and reignited for the impact and legacy you are meant to create in the world. You will be reminded of your own strength and challenged to dream a little bigger, fight a little harder for your dream, bounce back a little quicker when you get knocked down, and never ever give up because someone else is waiting on you to show up. There is nothing ordinary or average about who you are destined to be. You are meant to unleash your unique brilliance and be a beacon of light to others in the world. That is what you will be reminded of in this book.

I celebrate each of the co-authors of the Unleash Your Undeniable Impact book project for selflessly sharing their testimonies and messages of inspiration and empowerment. Each message will propel you to develop a new mindset, attitude, behaviors and patterns in order to unleash your undeniable impact, live your best life, and create legacy. As you immerse yourself in the Unleash Your Undeniable Impact book, you will be reminded that your impact matters and the world needs you!

Dr. Cheryl Wood
Compilation Visionary of Unleash Your Undeniable Impact
WEBSITE: www.cherylempowers.com
EMAIL: info@cherylwoodempowers.com
SOCIAL MEDIA: @CherylEmpowers

Allison Denise Arnett

"Trust the timing of your life."

UNKNOWN

Mini 3: Mommy! Mommy! My tooth is wiggling. When it moves like this, that means it's coming out!!!

Me: Awesome! Yes! Don't mess with it. Let it do its thing.

Mini 3: Maybe it's because I've been messing with it.

Me: Or maybe it's just time.

You're reading this because for you... it's just time. It's time for you to increase in love, wealth, health, and happiness. Time for the gifts stirred up in you to shine forth. Time for you to step in and possess your land. Time for you to see the promises of God spring forth in your life. Time to blaze your trail.

Not because you feel ready or because you've taken all the right steps in the right way but because God says it's time. How do I know that? A better question is, how do you know? Something tells me that you've started seeing the signs; the movement. The people, places, and things around you are shifting... moving in and out of place, maybe even seemingly out of control. Pay attention and trust God.

And while God is pleased when we meet our faith with actions, be careful not to think that it's happening because of something you did in your own power. No, God is in the center and is the shifter of it all. And guess what? He says when the time is right; He makes it happen. Check out Isaiah 60:22 in the Bible. This means you don't have to coerce, force, or manipulate anything or anyone. While you do what you've been instructed or inspired to do, things will fall in place in a mind-blowing serendipitous type of way.

According to Jeremiah 29:11, there is a plan for your life. A plan is a detailed map, decided in advance about how something will take place. Plans include steps set to happen in a certain order and timing. The timing will never seem just right to you, but God is a planner, and His timing is impeccable. The shift you are feeling is not coincidental. That stirring in your belly is not what you just ate. It's an exciting signal that is saying, "Jump! It's time!"

It's time to stop watching the clock and step into your moment. The hour has come for you to decide. Will you shift, or will you shrink? The minute you take that first step, you begin to take hold of your future.

The shifts happening in your life are part of the plan to make sure you unleash your undeniable impact on the world, and they are working for your good. I promise that provision is on the other side of your fear. So resist the fear. Be excited for change! "Behold, I do a new thing! Do you not see it! Says the Lord." Isaiah 43:19. Do you agree with God? Yes? Ok, then prove it. Clock in and put in the work.

Allison Denise Arnett

Allison Denise is a 9x Best Selling Author, International Speaker, and Award-Winning Graphic Designer of beautiful boss brands and books through her biz Brand It Beautifully™. A servant leader at heart and an eclectic, creative soul, she seeks to help Christian women in business stir up their gifts, monetize their message, edify the Body, and leave their legacy in the world. As an avid advocate of self-acceptance and spiritual empowerment, it is her desire that every woman finds the power in their voice and the beauty in her story. Every book she publishes, event she hosts, or class she teaches is part of her vision from God to merge ministry and the marketplace into one. She prays that something you experience, someone you meet, or something you do as a result of this encounter will ignite the fire in you to Empower Your Inner Creator™ and become everything God designed you to be.

Social Media @ImAllisonDenise
www.AllisonDeniseMinistries.com

Shawnta M. Ball

"Lives and careers have been known to change just from someone imparting and receiving a little here and a little there."

SHAWNTA M. BALL

This message is for anyone who feels stuck in any form or capacity. Whatever step you are on, you are not alone. Whatever step you are on is not your final step! It ain't over until you have taken your last breath. And even then, let the legacy live on.

A quadriplegic person has usually received an awful diagnosis from a doctor telling them that they will never walk again. It is said that of those with neck injuries who can only feel light touch, about one out of eight may eventually walk. The sooner the muscles start working again after a spinal cord injury, the better the chances of recovery for walking.

Like with anything else in life, we have to want it bad enough to go after it. Yes, you gotta be hungry for it! It takes having the mental strength and the capacity to start, finish and win. We must have a fighting spirit. Yes, we get knocked down sometimes, but let's not stay down too long.

There is greatness inside of you that needs to be released to the world. What's down on the inside of you are gifts that lead to living the life you really want. You have a testimony somebody needs to hear. Somebody needs to know where you came from and how you moved into greatness. Our stories and testimonies are bigger than us.

It is one thing to stay stuck in the place we're in, but it is an altogether wonderful thing when we encourage and strengthen ourselves with the help of the Lord to get up from where we have laid for far too long and walk into our destiny. Regardless of the reason for the setback or the delay, you can do this. Yes, I am telling you to get up! It is a matter of life and urgency! We must have resilience in the face of adversity, chaos, and confusion, the mental strength of a conqueror, and an attitude that says I shall not be greatly moved!

Be that walking miracle that inspires others! People will get up because they saw you get up and walk again. Let's be a walking demonstration, which shows people that although we have been hit with some hard knocks and steady blows, we got up. And not only did we get up, but we put the broken pieces together! We even found some of the lost pieces to the puzzle that were missing.

Patrick Rummerfield is the first spinal cord injury quadriplegic in history to recover full physical mobility. I encourage you to read his story. Today, he has numerous athletic accomplishments and works as a motivational speaker. If he can get up from being physically paralyzed, you can unlock your mind and move forward and upward. You are that giant ray of hope for somebody else! You are the answer to someone's prayer.

JESUS got up so that we all could get up! GET UP and WALK it out!

Les Brown and Dr. Cheryl Wood

Shawnta M. Ball

Ms. Shawnta M. Ball is the CEO of The Empress Sphere, LLC; Founder and President of the I Shall Live And Not Die Writes of Passion, Inc. (The ISLAND WOP) Non-Profit; author of HE Caught Your Tears, The Father of Mended Hearts; Forty Days and Forty Nights with the Saviour and Minister of Music, FWH; and Expect the Manifestation.

Shawnta is also featured as a co-author in the books, The Power of Sisterhood; and Unleash Your Undeniable Impact, which is a collaboration with International Motivational Speaker Dr. Cheryl Wood and the incomparable, world renown, Motivational Speaker, Mr. Les Brown (Mamie Brown's Baby Boy).

Shawnta is mom to one daughter, Angel, whom she cherishes and loves spending quality time with. Her passion for writing and storytelling is her life's work, along with being an instrumental mouthpiece and yielded vessel with her life for her Lord and Saviour.

www.EmpressSphere.com
EmpressFHG@gmail.com
@EmpressBall

Inspirational Message by
Barbara J. Beckley

"...You may not control all the events that happen to you, but you can decide not to be reduced by them."

MAYA ANGELOU

First, I want to start by saying that every individual has a purpose in life. We are created in this world to make a difference, to make a change; I know sometimes you might not feel like it. But we were designed to be an example for others to help them move forward, but you must dig deep inside and understand your story in your life is your golden stairway to leading and guiding yourself and others to that lighthouse of hope.

We all have our stories, the good, the bad, and the ugly; mine started from the age of 8 years old when I was bullied every day and told that I did not have a purpose and was not valued. Then, after losing a significant person in my life, my dad, my rock, was murdered when I turned 17," another stepping stone of courage. My life took another turn in my twenties. I was abused by a man that thought my no meant yes, another stepping stone of courage. Then just ten years ago, the doctor told me that I had uterine cancer and had an urgent hysterectomy.; I had to live with the fact that I would never have children in my lifetime, another stepping stone of courage.

I tell these stories of my life because these are badges of honor, not of a victim mentality" The purpose of why things happen in your life is to build you up to be an influencer, a connector to that lighthouse of hope. Leading by example is to go to the next stage in your life. We must take that next step of understanding when things happen; we should be rejoicing because it gives us another skill, increasing strength, and another story to help save somebody else's life.

I put out a challenge for every person that reads this chapter. Ask yourself when you decide in life. Make sure that your mindset and your heart set are coming together, and that will give you a good indicator that you are making the right decision to move forward and help others. Suppose your stories are sitting and you are not communicating with others. You are wasting a special badge of honor you proved to yourself that you could get through the valleys and come out on the other side with. It would be disrespectful not to share with somebody who might be going through something similar, and you can be that lighthouse to their hope.

Be proud of who you are, what you have become, and where you are going because you are an influencer, you are a conqueror, you are a monument of life and a pillar of hope for others that need to have that connection, so they know they are the next in line to lead by example.

Barbara J. Beckley

Barbara J. Beckley is a Professional Speaker, 7X Best Selling Amazon Author, Purpose, and Social Media Strategist and TV Host and Producer.

She is the founder and CEO of Diamond Factor LLC. The mission is to empower individuals to understand their PPD (Purpose, Passion, and Drive) and overcome their challenges to shine like a Diamond to the world. Barbara's motto is "Because everyone has something special within them, the Diamond Factor" as your foundation to encourage you to move forward despite the trials and challenges in your life.

Barbara offers promo interviewing to help individuals increase their visibility within their business, content coaching, webinar training, One-on-one coaching, seminars, TV Streaming, video production" and social media workshops.

Website: www.barbarabeckley.com

Inspirational Message by
Attiyah Blair

"Action is the activator."

ATTIYAH BLAIR

*I*t's time to hit the reset button!

If you are not making the amount of money you want to make, there is one reason why! You are not solving enough problems for enough people. And if you want large amounts of money, you have to solve large problems. People will pay you large sums of money to solve their problems, to help them reach their goals with less money, less time, and less stress. Even if they have to pay you large sums of money to do so, they are happy when you show up to solve their problem.

In 2016, I only made $25,000 a year as an entrepreneur. In 2018, I made about $80,000. But last month, I experienced an $80,000 day. You heard me right. $80,000 in just one day. When it happened, I couldn't help but think to myself, "I dreamed of days like this. I worked so hard for days like this. I prayed and cried and lost sleep to experience days like this." This is important to note for two reasons:

Reason 1: I made $80,000 in a day in my mind long before it showed up in my bank account. Yes, you have to fantasize about that number that you want. Some scientists believe that our brains can't tell the difference between fantasy and reality. Fantasizing about what you want makes it real.

Reason 2: The second reason I want to note this is because social media will have you thinking that something is wrong with you because you didn't achieve your money goals in a year. It will have you thinking everyone is an overnight success except you. It took me ten years to become an overnight success. I had to share that so you know there is nothing wrong with you. You are exactly where you need to be, and if you are willing to hit the reset button, you too can build the life of your dreams.

Building something great is not easy. To endure the hard days, you will need to have a why and hold onto it tightly. I reach my goals because I am insatiable with my success. I reach my goals because my purpose calls me, and I answer. I reach my goals because I'm very clear about my purpose, and I'm very clear that I will fulfill my purpose before I leave this earth if I don't do anything else. I'm going to give my all. My grave will be empty when it's my time to go because I'm going to share everything I've got with the world. That is my why. That is what allows me to endure the hardship.

My question to you is, what is your why? The answer can't be money. It has to be deeper than that! Fantasize about the lifestyle you want for yourself and your loved ones. That will lead you to your why. Hit the reset button and build the life of your dreams.

Attiyah Blair

Attiyah Blair is a multi-millionaire real estate investor, a mentor, and a licensed realtor. Attiyah's company, The Real Estate Reset, breathes life into severely distressed properties and turns them into beautiful homes. The company also provides jobs for members of the community. Attiyah has been investing in real estate since 2007 when she was only 23 years old, and is passionate about sharing her wealth-building knowledge with women and other aspiring real estate investors. Attiyah's signature mentorship program teaches her students "How to Build A Million Dollar Real Estate Portfolio in One Year." Before becoming a real estate investor, Attiyah worked for NBC, CBS, and FOX News for ten years. I share free real estate investing strategies on Instagram @AttiyahBlair. Also, you can check out my Free Masterclass at TheRealEstateReset.com.

Inspirational Message by
Deborah Flemming Bradley

"It's important for you to understand that your experience facing and overcoming adversity is actually one of your biggest advantages."

MICHELLE OBAMA

Waking up in your prosperity should be your priority. Every day when you wake up, you should feel richer in life. I am not talking about money rich, but that feeling of I came to win, I came to unleash my brilliance, my inner spirit, and all things that make me powerful in life.

You woke up today because some important work needed to be done. Work that will transform lives and give life to those who face the same challenges as you. The only difference is you can show the world what is on the other side of adversity. You bring your authentic self to every table set before you. Your self-confidence is undisputable because "what you see is what you get" is presented to every single person that crosses your path. On the outside, you are an imperfect and flawed vessel. On the inside, there is a mixture of your emotions and character that are in perfect harmony.

This is why it is so important for you to share, show and shock the world with your story. Sharing was never easy for me. I was taught to keep my personal issues behind closed doors. I would be screaming on the inside and angry on the outside because I wasn't releasing my pain or my joy.

Then one day, someone asked me, "Who are you?" and I told them my name, mother, wife, and businesswoman. The person asked me again, "Who are you?" and I told them that I like dancing, watching movies and social events. The person asked me again, "So, who are you?" and that's when I rattled off more things about myself and realized that I am more than what I thought I was. At that moment, I became insanely in LOVE with myself and who I was becoming.

When I shared my story, I showed others that we all have something in common. Our experiences are not our own. They are designed to show someone that whatever it is, you can overcome and achieve what the heart desires. I shocked everyone with my transparency and my vulnerability. When people found out that I was not an exception to hurt, pain, and loss, it helped them know that I could feel and see them.

Whether you know it or not, it is evident in the way you operate with certainty. Your actions are unquestionable because you have a strong faith in yourself and a higher being. You flourish because you are undeniable! There is no one like you. Your path is a zig-zag of twists and turns. When obstacles were in your way, you maneuvered with your heart and intuition, leading you to where you are today.

It takes a lot of heart to be you. No one can fight your fight like you. You have been knocked down but not knocked out. Look at you! You are winning in all rounds of life!

Deborah Flemming Bradley

Deborah Flemming Bradley holds a bachelor's degree in Public Relations and Marketing from the University of South Carolina School of Journalism and Mass Communications with a minor in Spanish. She currently serves as Co-Director of the PlanNet Cares Foundation and as a member of the National Association of Black Journalists, ColorComm, and the Public Relations Society of America. Through continued education, Deborah received a certificate of completion for Crisis Management through the Public Relations Society of America. Born and raised in Columbia, South Carolina, Deborah is proudly married to Donald Bradley and mother to four adult children, Brandon, Brian, Bryce, and Brooke. She resides in Atlanta, Georgia.

For more information, please visit her website at www.deborahflemmingbradley.com or connect on IG and FB @DeborahFlemmingBradley

Inspirational Message by
Kimberly M. Branche

"Each of us must confront our own fears, must come face to face with them. How we handle our fears will determine where we go with the rest of our lives. To experience adventure or to be limited by the fear of it."

JUDY BLUME

What's holding you back from doing the very thing you know you are called to do? Is it fear of rejection, fear of success, or maybe you lack confidence? Fear, according to Oxford, is "an unpleasant emotion caused by the belief that someone or something is dangerous, likely to cause pain or a threat." That four-letter word has caused so many individuals to not reach their full potential in life because they were afraid of an outcome that has not taken place. Can you imagine? I can relate to being a people pleaser, perfectionist, and worrying about what others would say about me. I let so many years go by trying to create a "fail-proof plan" that I almost missed my purpose in life.

See, fear will keep you from walking with confidence but dismay. There is no time to walk in fear and leave your purpose undiscovered and untapped. My brother used to say there were so many unfulfilled dreams buried in graves because people were too afraid to maximize their full potential. When we do not reach our full potential we cannot make an undeniable impact in life. It did not happen overnight for me as it took some time; a mindset shift change, confidence, and changing my inner circle. You must speak things into existence and change your mindset and know you are a conqueror. You have the power inside of you. So, what if the plan did not work? You get up, and you try again and again. Ask yourself, do you want to make an impact? It's your time to take the journey of walking in confidence over fear. You, my friend, it is time for you to activate F.E.A.R "Face Everything And Rise."

First, you must identify what is holding you back and why. When you identify it then and only then will you be able to work on a solution and the steps you need to take to conquer that fear. You must stop any self-doubt and negative talk. Again, change will not occur overnight, but with a mindset change, you can begin walking in VICTORY and activating F.E.A.R with confidence. You have a gift that needs to be used. Someone is waiting on what you have to say. You are the only person that has the power to change the narrative of your story. Nelson Mandela said, "I learned that courage was not the absence of fear, but the triumph over it. The brave man is not he who does not feel afraid, but he who conquers the fear." What are you going to do now that you know that you are brave enough to succeed to make an undeniable impact?

Kimberly M. Branche is a certified John Maxwell Coach, Entrepreneur, author, and Veteran. She has served alongside the military as a federal employee for 25 years empowering and mentoring young airmen and civilians. She holds a BS in Social Psychology and MA in Marriage and Family Counseling. She has combined both education and experience to encourage, motivate, and inspire women to stop walking in fear and heal from the past.

Kimberly is a Myositis warrior, Multiple Myeloma cancer survivor, and advocate. After her cancer diagnosis, she launched Branche Basu Boutique, a natural product line to educate consumers on wellness and self-care.

Kimberly is a contributing author of the #1 Best Selling book Destined To Win and Survivors Take A Real Stage. She has been featured on Good Morning Arizona, Air Force News and delivered speaking engagements on cancer survivorship.

For more information about Kimberly, go to www.kimberlybranche.com

Inspirational Message by
Angela Brand

"Release the fire and set a trail for others to follow!"

ANGELA BRAND

H ave you ever heard a speaker that was so good it caused the hairs on your arm to rise or something within you to leap of joy and excitement? Each word that came out of their mouth was like fire that went through your entire body. You sat on the edge of your seat, waiting on what they said next.

Have you ever wondered how they developed that skill? What techniques did they use to speak like that? I do; I call it speaking with power and passion. As a speaker, I have learned to tap into a fire within me that cannot be denied or contained.

The more I spoke, the more the fire stirred up. The more I dug into my purpose, the more the fire stirred up. The more I thought about the women waiting to hear me, the more the fire stirred up. The more I thought I wasn't good enough, the more the fire stirred up. The more I wanted to shrink back, the more the fire stirred.

If you are reading this, you have that same fire in your belly waiting to burst through you. My goal is to show you how to unleash your undeniable impact by tapping into that fire. I introduce to you the Fire Speaking Method.

Femininity is not a gender; it's an energy. This energy is designed to create, give life, open, and invite. Your speech should be presented in a way that creates an atmosphere that will cause them to dream again, have hope again, and open to a whole new world. This takes a level of skill but is effective because your job is to open your audience to new possibilities and show them what they can do if they believe in themselves.

Impact your listeners in a way that moves them to work with you. This level of impact has to be developed over time. Your product or service should be created for them to change or reach something they could not do on their own. Your impact is connected to the one thing no one else can do like you.

Rich content should teach the audience something they never knew. The richness of your speech is the glue your listeners need to piece their life back together. Without this, your speech is like an empty glass on a hot sunny day.

Extraordinary delivery leaves your audience in awe. I call this the "drop the mic effect." Average speakers miss this step and just close as everyone does. Extraordinary speakers leave the audience wanting more. This step guides the audience to rise above average and break the normal way of doing things.

Now take this fire and set a blaze in the world!

Angela Brand

Angela Brand is the CEO/Founder of Angela Brand Enterprise LLC, a one-stop-shop for author's coaches and speakers to learn how to "get paid" to be themselves by turning their mess into their message that will build leverage and influence. Angela is known as "The Girl on Fire," a Best-Selling author, women empowerment speaker, trainer, publisher, and personal branding coach. She has authored four book anthologies of her own and been a part of 4 others, and believes in leaving a legacy through her books for the next generation. She dedicates her life to train life coaches and motivational speakers, providing them with certifications through AB Coaching Academy. She will stop at nothing until she has done everything the Lord has sent her to earth to do and stand on "Living Full and dying empty."

www.angelabrandenterprise.com, @iamangelabrand

Inspirational Message by
Na'tosha L. Brooks

"We Don't Have Next, We Have Now!"

DR. BARBARA WILLIAMS-SKINNER

In a world that is ever-changing, filled with trials and tribulations and countless uncertainties, there is a moaning in the earth realm through the travail of the people because desperation has a sound. They are searching frantically for that someone who is equipped to ease the pain, extend hope and increase opportunities—the one in their prayers, dreams, and visions who can lead them to their triumphs.

SURPRISE...You Are The Gift they are awaiting with great anticipation to receive, unwrap and utilize, so please maneuver to your unveiling party and take your rightful place. The truth is that you are here on purpose and in purpose for such a time as this. You are necessary...You are needed. Yes, Y-O-U! The one who has noticeable flaws, has fallen down, fallen back, and failed numerous times in various areas of your personal and professional life. The one who may not have it all together but is equipped to encourage. The one who does not have a lot of money but has life's experiences to motivate. Simply point, it's your turn and your time. This is your season to conceive, carry and/or deliver what the Lord has deposited within you for the world's nourishment and His Glory. The due date has been set, and the alarm is ringing for you to proceed both forward and upward in faith. There is no space nor time for procrastination, nor the pressure of fear to paralyze you into preventing to produce all of your pregnant possibilities. Your private preparation determines your public pinning and promotion, so within each season, take proper inventory of your posture.

Oftentimes, we become subdued by society's standards leading to catastrophic chokeholds of comfort, competition, community opinions, and culture's conformity resulting in one's inability to breathe in their promises. We focus energy and efforts on familiarity, as well as, being man's favorite vs. God's favored, but not you! Why? Because you are cognizant of the approximate cost of what you being out of position will incur/entail, which cannot be pinpointed in an exact value because the specifics of just how many are awaiting you to move on your way so that they can find theirs, cannot be accurately measured. Dispel the mental myths. They are not looking for perfection; they are searching for the pureness of what you have to offer. It's the authentic alignment, whether directly or indirectly, that ushers open the door to trust and transformation.

It is your time to bear down, pray, pause, plan, and push to break out of your bondage and deliver your blessings so others can experience their breakthroughs!

May you become impregnated with a fiery hunger to become positioned within the womb of Education, Edification, and Excellence. The seeds of wisdom planted and your priceless investments have and shall yield a plentiful harvest for others to glean from and an influential global impact to be birthed. **CONGRATULATIONS!**

Na'tosha L. Brooks

Na'tosha L. Brooks is a proud mother, educator, activist, actress, speaker, co-founder of The Birthing Movement, Inc., High Point University's Office of Student Success Department Administrator, Alpha Kappa Alpha Sorority, Inc. member, servant leader in her community and Kingdom of God vessel passionate about edifying others while fighting oppression as a change agent. She is a former North Carolina Public School Special Educator, Teacher of the Year, and Director for Mount Zion Baptist Church of Greensboro, Inc.'s Afterschool and Summer Enrichment Programs.

A few of Na'tosha's accomplishments include recognition as NC Triad Business Journal's 40 Under 40 Leader, Fox8 News "Good For Her" segment feature, ACHI Magazine's Non-Profit Executive and Mentor of the Year nominee. She served as a Mentor for Triad Business Journal's Bizwomen Mentoring Monday and was recognized as a Success Women's Conference National Speaker and Influencer Nominee.

LinkedIn: Na'tosha Brooks | **Facebook**: Na'tosha Brooks | **Instagram**: @natoshab3

Inspirational Message by
Shamika Dokes-Brown

"Love recognizes no barriers. It jumps hurdles, leaps fences, penetrates walls to arrive at its destination full of hope."

MAYA ANGELOU

For years I allowed people in my life to define what I could achieve and what was attainable for me. Little did I know, every trial and tribulation I endured in life began to shave away the layers to reveal something I had struggled to name "intergenerational trauma."

Being able to trace my trauma back six generations has been eye-opening, healing, heartbreaking, and freeing. I saw how I was immersed in the same fear that clung to my mother like a spandex bodysuit. Yes, my mother was a fighter, but she too inherited fears from her mother. Out of fear, I struggled with allowing my voice to be heard. I stayed silent when I wanted to speak out. I had also been afraid to follow my heart's desire to travel and venture into the unknown.

I often think about the mighty women warriors, whose shoulders I stand upon—how there was a time when they had to receive approval to grieve the loss of their children or their loved ones, and how they had to grieve the loss of their dreams.

The mighty women warriors ran a race filled with stipulations that were made to limit them and keep them in fear. The rules of the race weren't created to be fair to them. The baton given to my ancestors was designed to stop them in their tracks, not to be passed forward.

To overcome the intergenerational trauma I inherited from this race, I had to go back for the baton that wasn't intended to make it to me and recover the crowns withheld from them. By nurturing my future, I found that I could heal and uproot the trauma of the past. The pain I carried gave way to responsibility and honor.

With the transformation of my mind, I saw that the mighty women warriors who came before me had superpowers that were priceless: resilience, love without borders, courage to stand in the middle of life's hurricanes and not bend, faith to believe the unseen, and strength to build. We all have these in common.

As I continue this journey, my destiny has become even clearer: I am created to be a healer and connect the dots for the generations that come after me. I do not need anyone's permission to walk in my calling or to deposit seeds of hope. Today, I can run forward in a new race with the strength I inherited from my ancestors, using my voice to proclaim stories of freedom that provide others with a roadmap to overcoming. Over the past 18 years, I have traveled across the nation and had the honor to support so many amazing women of various generations and ethnicities through the birthing of their children, dreams, life obstacles, and transitions.

I now pass you the baton.

Shamika Dokes-Brown

Shamika Dokes-Brown is a resilient innovator. As the business owner of Lena Mae's Bath and Beauty Boutique, Shamika has pressed through barriers and boundaries to attain what others believed were insurmountable goals. After her mother's death, she turned trauma, grief, and struggle into strength and determination. This fortitude was used to craft and produce her skin-loving products. Also, for over 18 years, Shamika remains committed to making a difference in Women's Health and Family Wellness.

Instagram: lenamaessoapboutique.
Please visit us online at http://lenamaesbathandbeautyboutique.com

Inspirational Message by
Dr. Trina Brown

"When we focus our energy towards constructing a passionate, meaningful life, we are tossing a pebble into the world, creating a beautiful ripple effect of inspiration. When one person follows a dream, tries something new or takes a daring leap, everyone nearby feels that energy and before too long they are making their own daring leaps and inspiring yet another circle."

CHRISTINE MASON MILLER

As a single mother, I have always felt that I needed to do more to provide for my son and me. But like everything else I knew then, I was working a regular 9 to 5 job trying to make ends meet. Until one day, I was talking to a co-worker, and he said, "you should look into working part-time as a loan officer for additional income, with your accounting knowledge." I responded, "Really, you think so?" And it was then when I tossed my pebble (the dream) into the world to create a ripple impact and started my journey of being self-employed. For two years, I worked my regular job and part-time as a loan officer. On May 1, 2001, I became a full-time entrepreneur, freeing myself from the inability to provide more for my family. This year I celebrate my 20th anniversary of being self-employed. When I started my business, I did not realize what was being released would have a ripple effect and save over 1800 families in 2008 from the mortgage crisis.

The ripple effect will allow you to unleash your unquestionable impact. As you read this chapter, think about tossing your pebble into the world and allowing it to create a ripple impact for you and others. One thing about a ripple effect is it starts off as if nothing happens. When you first throw the pebble in the water, there is no sign of movement. Then slowly, you see a sign of a small circle forming in the area you tossed the pebble. So, throw that thing which is deep within you. Then create your ripple effect, which might be launching that new business, writing a book that would inspire and motivate others, as well as a coach and a mentor to more people to create their impact in the world.

Sometimes it would seem as though the ripple has faded away, and you might begin to give up on your vision, but you must constantly create movement and walk into your PURPOSE. I had to encourage myself throughout this process, knowing that everything I needed was in me. I focused on my faith and listened to motivational speakers. You must release the restraint of a negative mindset that has come to deny you of making an impact on you, your family, and the world.

I want you to do this mental exercise with me. Close your eyes and imagine you are at the edge of the lake, and you have your pebble in your hands, which is your dream. Throw it into the water (the world). Now, stand there and then wait for the small circle to form and look at the continuation of the other circles. The very thing that you are holding in your hand is the key to your success, so release it into the world and watch the impact you make.

"Go Unleash your Undeniable Impact!"

Dr. Trina Brown

#1 Best Selling Author, has served the Communities as an Advocate for Healthcare and Humanity for over 30 years, International Motivational Speaker and Radio Host in over 180 countries, Mental and Healthy Lifestyle Coach, Mental Fitness Trainer, Inventor, Evangelist/ Prophetess, Founder/CEO Data Civility LLC (African American biomedical company) and Neuro Pathic Trainers Foundation, Inc. (Mental and Physical healthy lifestyle) a division of Dr. Trina Brown & Associates. Dr. Brown has been serving on numerous committees and ministered with various organizations. Dr. Brown's mission is to educate and empower people about healthcare issues with dementia and the financial impact on families and communities. "Power and Greatness within the M.I.N.D." Mental Improvement Negates Deterioration. Dr. Brown is a God-fearing woman who trusts the Lord. Dr. Brown is a mother of one son Fredrick Brown-Grant Jr. To learn more about Dr. Trina Brown, please visit her websites: www.neuropathictrainers.com and www.datacivility.com.

"Be your BEST, Do your BEST, & Give your BEST"

Inspirational Message by
Dr. Shamara L. Byrd

"Failure does not dictate your future, but failure to get back up does. See your failures as an opportunity to adjust your path, not abort your purpose."

DR. SHAMARA L. BYRD

As you stand and stare at yourself in the mirror, the woman looking back at you is beautiful, intelligent, confident, and courageous. Instead of celebrating her, your eyes are drawn to the tiny reflection of her mistakes, flaws, and failures off in the backdrop. You fight to re-frame this negative image, but that voice in your head tells you that you are not enough to manifest the vision God placed on the inside of you. Surprisingly, the voice sounds like yours. Feeling defeated, you turn and walk away from the mirror. Mission accomplished! Your mistakes and failures smile with gleam. You bought the lies of the enemy. As you turn and walk away from the mirror, not only did you give up on yourself, you gave up on the many people who are stuck, waiting for you to show up and throw them a lifeline.

I was once that woman staring in the mirror, rejecting the woman looking back. I could not see me as God sees me. I allowed my past to stop me from pursuing my passion and my divine purpose. I survived some storms and faced some unfavorable conditions. Being born into generational poverty, raised in a housing project in the inner city of Miami, Florida, I witnessed physical and emotional abuse between my parents, homeless, and molested by a family member. Not to mention dismissed by my daddy as he built a family that did not include me. The aftermath of these storms left me to face unfavorable conditions of low self-confidence, low self-worth, and fear of failure, rejection, and abandonment. Exposure to the unfavorable conditions and unhealed wounds as a child, manifested in my adult life. For years I was merely existing and not living. I masked my pain, silenced my voice, buried myself in obtaining multiple degrees, hoping to gain some sense of self-worth. I longed to be loved by a man hoping to fill the void of my father. As a result, I often compromised my standards and questioned my self-worth, resulting in heartbreak and me becoming a young single mother. But I refused to give up. I believed my failures did not dictate my future. I persevered through the pain, overcame obstacles, and used my faith to fight my fears and insecurities.

You may be in the very place I once stood, feeling like damaged goods. Fear of failure and low self-confidence keeps you stagnant, afraid to step out on faith and pursue that thing that you are passionate about. You cannot not see how your *imperfect* life could have a positive *impact* on anyone. Truth is you were created on purpose for a purpose and you have been equipped to fulfill that purpose. You may fall but you will not fail. As your creator, God has a vested interest in your success. It is time to birth the baby. No more hiding. No more doubting. When residue from your past shows up on your path and attempts to hold you back from reaching your intended destination, remember, you are not an accident. You were created on purpose, for a purpose, and God equipped you to fulfill that purpose. The mere fact that you are still here, in your right mind, is a clear indication that God has preserved you for a purpose. See yourself as God sees you. Step out, show up, speak up, and unleash your undeniable impact.

Dr. Shamara L. Byrd

Dr. Shamara L. Byrd is a multifaceted woman of God who lives her faith out loud daily as mother, educator, mentor, entrepreneur, motivational messenger, trainer, published author, and Christian Success Coach. Dr. Byrd firmly believes that the love of God, hope, faith and determination are the keys to living a life of peace, purpose, and prosperity. She is passionate about fulfilling her divine purpose of using her pain as the prescription for healing and breakthrough of women who are struggling to live successfully as single women or mothers. Women who are allowing their many mistakes, failed attempts, and imperfections to prevent them from pursuing their passion and fulfilling their divine purpose. As vehicles to reach women, Dr. Byrd founded D.I.V.A Coaching Academy and Byrd's Nest Outreach, Inc. Follow her at www.divacoachingacademy.com, @DIVACoachingAcademy on FB & IG and @byrdsnestorg on FB & IG.

Debra Bell-Campbell

"Don't allow humility to be your harness."

DEBRA BELL-CAMPBELL

Have you ever wondered what the world would be like if people like Maya Angelou, Mahatma Gandhi, or President Barack Obama had never roamed the earth? If their impact was never realized? Each of these people moved about the world with a sense of ease and purpose. Each experienced hardship that many of us will only read about. I have always found people fascinating, as we often look beyond ourselves to find the strength to carry on. I challenge you today to reach within and confirm that you do not have to be your version of Maya Angelou, Mahatma Gandhi, or President Barack Obama to be impactful. All you must do is be authentically you.

All my life, I have had to bob and weave through the shadows of my siblings. You see, I am number eight of 12 siblings, and figuring out where I fit was truly my challenge. Perhaps, fitting in has been your challenge as well. Fitting in is not only about belonging but also acceptance. When you have so many people in line for your queen's attention, someone typically gets left out. As an introvert, I always had the answers yet was challenged with "spitting" it out fast enough. Have you ever heard of the phrase, "the early bird gets the worm?" Well, I learned quickly that if I wanted something, I had to beat the others to it—that required strategic planning. However, I want to caution you to be aware of the habits of a humble person, like being situationally aware or putting other people first. Do not allow these traits and others to be the harness to keep you from going after your dreams.

As an introverted international speaker, 3x best-selling author, and master life coach, I can tell you that the road to success is not paved in gold. It takes a tremendous amount of work to decide to become that which you know you have been called to be. So, it does not matter where you have been, yet it matters where you intend to go. You must have a vision for your life. I encourage you to keep going no matter what. You may never know how your decision to embrace yourself will impact others. Moreover, the world is waiting for you to show up. Every moment you deny your gift, someone fails to move forward.

Ultimately, if you aspire to be your absolute best, you must **S.H.I.F.T. (Stop Hiding Inside and Face Your Truth).** Here are three strategies that you can use to help you maximize your vision and dominate your life:

Believe in yourself: You are uniquely you. Never be afraid to dream a bigger dream.

Promote yourself: It is time to level up. Release your fears and do it anyway.

Be authentically you: Never compromise yourself to meet anyone else's perception of you.

If you are ready to make the S.H.I.F.T., connect with me @ dbellcampbell@yahoo.com

Debra Bell-Campbell

As one of the most sought-after introverted women leadership experts, Debra Bell-Campbell is an MBTI Certified Practitioner, National Certified Counselor, Wellness Coach, 2x Best-Selling Author, and International Speaker. With over 15 years of coaching women in leadership in private and corporate settings, she has designed, developed, and delivered exceptional programs to promote and enhance professional and personal growth. She is passionate about helping her clients revel in their success in a "true to you" nature and reminding clients to embrace the mind and body connection to summon their inner strength and annihilate all barriers to success. Ultimately, every client must **S.H.I.F.T.** (**Stop Hiding Inside, & Face Your Truth**).

Did we mention Debra has designed and delivered programs for The National Weather Service and various State Departments in Florida? She takes her clients on a journey to embrace their superhero within and garner comprehensive business solutions.

Visit her at www.debrabell-campbell.com.

Tammy J. Carpenter

"The danger in experiencing perceived freedom is
feeling content and never pursuing true freedom."

TAMMY J. CARPENTER

Wrapped, tied, tangled… almost mummified, but there are definite
signs of life. It's your Lazarus experience, except no one is running
to the Savior, wishing He had been present to intercept what got you to
this state. You have functioned and even produced from this place, so
no one recognizes the death of YOU. Could it be that you've never really
lived, and the glimpses of LIFE you've seen appear to be unattainable
or not acceptable for you? This was my existence. Please allow me to
encourage YOU as I share a glimpse into my path of walking free.

I grew up as what I would consider a "church girl," and as an adult, I continued in that mindset and adopted supporting behaviors. No one would
have been able to convince me that I wasn't living the ultimate purpose
for my life until one Sunday morning, it all changed. I received a message with the words, "I am no longer your Pastor; send your keys…."
That text was my notice of being excommunicated from the community
my life revolved around. My world as I knew it was shattered, and I was
lost. Unbeknownst to me at the time, that incident was necessary. In
hindsight, it was one of the best things to happen to me, and it was the
beginning of my unleashing. For almost ten years, I served diligently
in someone else's dream and was convinced that it was my own. I was

tightly wrapped and covered in layers of the approval of others and their words that accompanied their fickle applause.

Fortunately, I had a "come forth" experience like Lazarus, and the layers had to "loose me and let me go." The unexpected rescue called me from a tomb of merely existing, freed me from a mummified state, and positioned me to breathe freely and truly begin to LIVE. That's when the process of learning that I was undeniable began for me. I embarked on a journey of discovering a plan and a purpose for my life that already has a "Yes!" attached to it. A journey of fully trusting God's plan. A journey to believing that I am enough and, like you, I'm undeniable. A journey to ME, authentically.

I call YOU forth. You show up for others regularly. However, you can't recall the last time you recognized YOU. You have a starring role, responding to every cry for an encore, and it's never enough. Your best performance will never be enough on a stage where you move solely based on external cues, and you've lost sight of the original script. You feel void of LIFE. We're serving notice to every layer formed by the expectations of others to loose you and let you go. You have always been enough to fulfill the plan purposed for your life. You are unleashed! Breathe in this fresh air of freedom, stretch beyond imputed limitations and enjoy the stroll on this new journey. Welcome to Y.O.U. - Your Own Undeniableness.

Tammy J. Carpenter

Tammy Carpenter discovered her love for equipping and empowering others over 20 years ago when she began her career as a Software Consultant. Her profession connects with her passion and faith as she aspires to share truths to inspire.

Tammy is a published author, a licensed Minister, and the Founder of the non-profit organization enLife, which offers programs to help women succeed through transition. Tammy helps authors bring life to their vision by offering consulting services through her business, Effectual Concepts.

Tammy is certain that one of her assignments is to help women celebrate their journeys. Using her brand name, Simply Tammy, she hosts the Women Who Win vodcast interviewing women who transparently share their journey to inspire others.

Tammy is most grateful to God for transforming her life, and that fuels her desire to share God's love with others through various mediums. Connect and learn more at http://simplytammy.com.

Inspirational Message by
Troy Carroll

"It is never too late to be what you might have been."

GEORGE ELIOT

I am going to tell you a secret.

Even though I have never met you…. I know your purpose.

Are you ready to hear it?

Alright…here goes….

Each of us was meant to be as great….as we intend to be.

That is it.

That is your purpose.

Simple and easy, right?

Well…. not always.

Then again…success rarely is.

Adversity happens. Obstacles and mountains appear out of nowhere to tell you, "Do not pass…."

But here is the thing….

Those obstacles… and the mountains that come with them... are a part of the journey, regardless of whether you like it or not.

Climb…

You see…life is not always easy nor fair, and yet, despite those facts, it is in those moments, with those mountains, that you become the best version of who you were meant to be.

In 1967 Marvin Gaye and Tammi Terrell released "Ain't No Mountain High Enough."

This song, which was a number one hit twice, spoke of a love so strong that nothing could stand in its way.

Maybe it's time to apply that same determination to the *"Mountains"* of adversity that crop up in our lives.

It does not matter the height or the width of the obstacle; nothing should keep you from getting **Through** and *TO* your *"Meant to be."*

Climb….

Yes, sometimes our journey to success can be a mountain of adversity and setbacks, and too often, we stand at the base of those mountains and say…

"How am I supposed to get over that?"

First….don't make a mountain out of a molehill. Take a deep breath, remember why you are here, keep moving.

Second…the **"MOUNTAIN"** is not there to mock you…nor stop you.

It is there to motivate you.

When you feel as if it is too big or too high, ask yourself….

"Do I intend to be the best version of who I was meant to be?"

The answer should always be

"Yes…."

Third…. "How do I get to the top?"

Climb….

One step and one handhold at a time.

If, for some reason, you decided to stand at the bottom, wringing your hands and saying, *"It's too hard."*

Remember.

This is **YOUR** mountain, and it will still be there regardless of whether you choose to climb it.

Or not.

It's there for a reason.
If you think…. *"I Can't,"*
Then….
You *"Won't."*

Now…you COULD stand at the bottom staring up at your *"Meant to Be,"* afraid to fall.
You will not get any closer to your goals, but you will avoid some pain.
Or you could…
Climb…

With every step, you will see and learn more about yourself than you have ever imagined.
Climb…
Understand that each pull on a handhold brings you ever closer to your best life.
Your best *"You."*

Your Mountain.
Your Risk.
Your Reward.
Climb…
At the top of that mountain, you will see other mountains.
Yes…more to do, but that's okay.
You were designed for this.

"Ain't no mountain high enough."

Climb…

Troy Carroll

Best-selling Author, Speaker, Certified Life Coach, and Founder of InsideOut Evolution, Troy is a Motiv8tional Warrior who has purposely dedicated his life to helping others bridge the gaps of adversity.

With over 20 years as a Performance Improvement Specialist, Troy turned skills earned in the Corporate Workspace and leveraged them to help those in the Personal Life space.

He understands that a large part of being the best version of yourself and creating success in your life requires you to unpack your bag, define and refine the "Who in You" to discover your purpose, and then applying those lessons to your life.

Using Life Coaching and dynamic speaking skills, Troy helps clients navigate the sometimes choppy waters of life by helping them to understand their Purpose AND Passion.

"Success is an Inside job with Outside results. Persistence and Progress over Perfection."

www.insideoutevo.com

Inspirational Message by
Leona Carter

"The revelation you've been given is for the impartation you'll be pouring."

LEONA CARTER

When I was going through rough times in my marriage, I didn't know if or when I would see daybreak in my relationship. I felt like I was drowning in a 50-foot ocean, but when I looked around, it was only 2-feet.

I desperately wanted a great marriage, but I was drowning because I did not have clarity or purpose. I did not understand what God was doing through me in my relationship. I question why He didn't save me from the nightmare I found myself startled from each night.

As soon as I thought I was coming up for air, I leave my doctor's office with three diagnoses and 13 medications, including a shot in my stomach every single day for the next seven years. Those numbers did not add up to my destiny, so I thought.

I am here to tell you I was being unleashed to the undeniable impact I was getting ready to make on marriages around the globe. As an intimacy coach, I shared my story around the world, including in Paris, France. Because of that, women shared their stories with tears for the first time in their life, to me.

When I learned my story was bigger than me, I allowed God to show up in my weakness so that I could be the strength for someone else. I empowered women who were being overtaken in the 2-foot ocean, like I was, and reached for her hand. I was able to encourage another woman to let her know she's not going to drown.

When you are in the midst of the pain that tries to wrap its arms around you, I need you to know the purpose of the pain is bigger than you. I know it seems like you are the only one feeling the pain, but that's how you will be able to talk someone else through the pain.

When you unleash your undeniable impact, you walk in your destiny singing, "All I do is win, win, win no matter what!"

When you unleash your undeniable impact, you realize your story is for somebody in the room.

When you unleash your undeniable impact, you will know when to say yes and when to say no.

When you unleash your undeniable impact, the question changes from which TV show I should watch to which TV show I should host.

When you unleash your undeniable impact, you don't operate FOR acceptance; you operate FROM acceptance.

When you unleash your undeniable impact, you're no longer bothered when people talk about you because they lost the ability to talk to you.

It's time to unleash your undeniable impact **now**! Tomorrow is not promised. Someone is waiting for the solution you provide today.

Leona Carter

Leona Carter empowers women to build intimacy with their husbands through the power of dating again to enhance communication, from the kitchen to the bedroom. Leona is an International Empowerment Speaker, Multi-best-selling Author, and Intimacy Coach. As the President and CEO of Carter Strategies, Leona hosts, Hey Coach Carter TV, where she talks to married women who are building their business and their bedroom without sacrificing either one.

Married since 1995, Leona, and her high school sweetheart, Omarr, have six children and one grandson. Leona and her family moved from Seattle, Washington, to Kalamazoo, Michigan, for the tuition-based program called The Kalamazoo Promise, where her family was featured in the New York Times.

Leona's energetic personality and vibrancy set her apart from the normalcy of entrepreneurship. She blazes a trail everywhere she goes through her passion for serving. Connect with Leona at http://www.leonacarter.com.

Inspirational Message by
Mayra Figueroa-Clark LICSW

"You alone are ENOUGH. You have nothing to prove to anybody."

MAYA ANGELOU

*I*t wasn't until recently that this quote is so real for my life. See, I always believed I needed to be strong, be there for others, hold it down. And for years, I was able to… seamlessly. I was able to hold space for friends, family even colleagues. From infidelity, death, job loss, depression, suicide, and miscarriages; with little disruption to my daily life. I mean, I am a therapist. But more than that, I always felt like I needed to be there for others. Have you ever felt like this? Have you ever felt that you "Had" to be strong for others? Carry their burden even when it was heavier than you ever thought?

That while you're carrying others' burdens, you find yourself alone? Having no one to turn to, because well, "they are busy" and you don't want to bother them? Yea, well, me too. And it all came crashing down in 2019 for me.

2019 was an exceptionally tough year. Political decisions affected my immigrant clients. I was living vicariously through them. My extended family was hurting; physically, financially. There were struggles all around, and I took them on. I attempted to ease struggles for others, support family members in crisis. Yet struggled to live my own life. My eating was out of control. I didn't sleep well, and my finances were in disarray. Still, I kept moving forward as if I owed someone something. I preached self-love and self-care. However, I wasn't practicing it. I stopped getting my monthly massages, my own therapist moved back to her country, and I didn't search for a new one. I didn't stay still for longer than a minute to check in with myself and my capacity.

Then in the late Fall of 2019, I felt sick. I had a cough that didn't go away. I went to a doctor for my flu-like symptoms. My new doctor found my blood pressure so high that I could have had a stroke any moment. She tried to stay calm, but I can tell something was going on. I had never been diagnosed with high blood tension nor ANY chronic disease. I was scared yet still felt terrible from the 'flu.' My physician placed me on bed rest for a week. Then two weeks, then four weeks.

I had never been so sick, never been on sick leave. Yet, this was the time where I was at capacity. My mind, body, and soul said STOP!!! Slow down, take care of me!!! You ALONE are enough. You don't have to prove to anyone you are great or loving or caring or able. You are ENOUGH. The love you give and how much you can give at that specific time is Enough. Your time is enough.

First, take care of yourself. Remind yourself that YOU ARE ENOUGH. Take care of that little girl inside of you that needs your every attention. Love her, believe in her, see her. You ALONE ARE ENOUGH!!!!

Mayra Figueroa-Clark LICSW

Mayra Figueroa-Clark, LICSW, is passionate about dispelling the Mental Illness Stigma and elevating Mental Health professionals. As a clinical psychotherapist, she empowers individuals, small groups, and couples using experimental workshops, overcoming trauma through a mindfulness lens, EMDR, Cognitive-behavioral therapy (CBT), Systems Theory, and psychoeducation. She offers therapy for individuals and small groups who may be grappling with anxiety, depression, work-life balance, executive functioning, and stress management. She also works with children and adolescents grappling with anxiety and depression.

Throughout her 24 years of clinical work, Mayra is compassionate and bold. She often uses practical strategies with the foundation of a strength-based philosophy and through a trauma lens. Her professional experience spans many disciplines. She is proud of her private practice and especially enjoys facilitating trainings/workshops on trauma-informed practices and Vicarious Trauma (Self-care for the caregiver), to name a few.

To connect with her, please email figueroaclark.m@gmail.com or https://mayra-figueroa-clark.clientsecure.me/

Carolyn Brooks-Collins

"...To be a butterfly, you must want to fly so much that you are willing to give up being a caterpillar."

TRINA PAULUS

W e as women are often carried by the waves of life doing what others expect of us - we grow up, go to school, focus on our careers, get married, then start taking care of our families. It's an age-old story that can become a vicious cycle. We live our lives for others, often in a cocoon of comfort and conformity designed by others. We forget, or perhaps never give ourselves permission, to dream or believe that God has ordained us to live purposefully - to inspire and impact others. But often, we stay in that familiar cocoon, wondering if it is too late to dream. Is it too late for me to discover my divine purpose on this earth?

I totally understand this because these are questions I asked myself. After raising my family and spending 45 years in Corporate America in the Accounting arena, I had to ask if that was all there was to life. I knew I lived a suitable life, and perhaps even a good life, but it was not my best life. I had become comfortable playing the role of supporting cast member in my own life versus being the star! You know most people never achieve their dreams or recognize their talents because they are just like some of us – unaware of our possibilities, afraid to take a step out of our comfort zones. We let fear of the unknown and fear of failure keep us where we are, in that seemingly safe and protected space.

My mother used to say, "Never be afraid of change. What's the worst that could happen? If you fall down, then just get up, dust yourself off, and keep on going." Those words have sustained me throughout my life. I remembered them when I left a failed marriage in my early 20's that everyone except me thought was perfect and again when I lost my job due to downsizing and my husband to his battle with lung cancer in my 50's. However, I remembered them again in my 60's when I FINALLY gave myself permission to think about my goals and dreams and became a motivational speaker. I took control of my life and stopped letting life control me.

My message is that it's time to emerge from the cocoon, be fearless, find your own purpose and build your own dreams. Unleash your undeniable impact on the world! Know that when you choose purpose over fear, you will win every time! As Roy T. Bennett said, "…on the other side of fear lies freedom…." It is the freedom to take control of your life and write that next chapter about the marvelous power within you to effect change in yourself and others! Everyone is waiting for your story! Structure your thoughts to access the greatness within you that will lead you to an extraordinary life, have an impact on others, and leave a legacy! "You have greatness and unlimited potential in you," Les Brown.

Carolyn Brooks-Collins

Carolyn Brooks-Collins, owner and founder of M. Carolyn Brooks-Collins LLC, encourages people to follow their dreams.

Carolyn understands women often defer their dreams and goals due to life's challenges and priorities and is passionate about helping to empower them to transform their lives, step into their purpose and become financially independent. She is a Certified Speaker through the Power Voice program, developed and taught by the legendary motivational speaker, Mr. Les Brown. She is a graduate of the Proctor Gallagher Institute's "Thinking Into Results" Program, led by top PGI coach Mr. Jon Talarico. Carolyn is also a graduate of the Pathbuilder's Percepta Women's Leadership Development program in Atlanta, GA, where she currently resides. She serves on the Boards of two non-profit organizations and maintains her professional licenses as a CPA and CFE. She has a B.S. in Accounting and an MBA in Project Management.

Learn more at her website: carolynbrookscollins.com

Inspirational Message by
JJ Conway

"No one ever got rich by studying poverty
and thinking about poverty."

WALLACE D. WATTLES

In 2009, I came home from a military trip to find my house sold, my stuff thrown out, and divorce papers to sign. That week I became a single military mom with over $845,000 of debt to my name, most of which was taken (and spent) by my ex-husband.

People said to file bankruptcy. Walk away from my debts. "You'll never overcome that," they said. "It's too much!" they insisted. But back then, the only job I knew how to do required the highest military clearances, which would be taken from me if I filed bankruptcy. Besides, the people I knew who had filed for bankruptcy seemed to be in a never-ending cycle of debt and bankruptcy. I wanted better for my son!

I wanted better for my future!

I learned how to hustle in a hurry, working multiple businesses in addition to my military job. Instead of hiding from them, I ran toward my creditors, assuring them I would pay in full one day, even if I could only pay one or two dollars at the moment. I scoured the library and the internet and learned how to make money work for me.

This is how I discovered the power of wealth attraction.

Dumping debt and building wealth isn't just about how much money you make or how much you save. Those things are absolutely important, but they're not the KEY that unlocks your wealthy future.

The key is to unlock the wealth-attraction superpower hiding within you.

Each of us has enough energy, intellect, and talent to unleash this superpower. We've been so conditioned to poverty as a way of life that most of us never realize the latent power hiding in each of us. Anyone can break the cycle of generational poverty when they follow time-tested success strategies. These strategies are biblical principles, and I will give you the first one today:

Wallace Wattles taught that the hardest thing you'll ever do is stay focused on thinking about yourself as prosperous. This is the first step we must take to break the generational cycle of poverty and push back against a world that tells us we're worthless and will never be good enough. We must believe that we are worthy, constantly visualize ourselves as prosperous, and commit to our future. We do this by writing a detailed vision of what we want and including what we will give in exchange. We reflect on that vision at least twice a day, and we take daily consistent action in the direction of this dream.

It sounds simple until you try it. And because it sounds simple, many never try it. We may dream for a moment, but then the realities of life choke out our dreams. You must be persistent in visualizing your dream every day.

When we do, everything changes! Doors begin to open, and opportunity finds you. This is how you begin to break the cycle of generational poverty.

I believe in your power to create your future!

JJ Conway

Janine "JJ" Conway was the first African American to serve as a physicist in the Air Force, retiring as a Lieutenant Colonel after 23 years. She became a financial planner after returning from a military trip to discover her house sold, divorce papers, and over $845,000 debt to her name. JJ learned how to hustle and make money work for her quickly yet ethically. She now teaches others the same personal growth and financial management skills that allowed her to break the cycle of poverty and mirrors these principles when working with businesses to improve processes, people, and profit.

Free 28-Days to Financial Freedom Bootcamp: https://JJCLink.com/gift
Instagram: http://instagram.com/JJKnowsTheWay
Facebook, Twitter, LinkedIn, YouTube, Clubhouse @ JJKnowsTheWay

Inspirational Message by
Montrella Cowan, LICSW

"Anyone who is interested in making change in the world, also has to learn how to take care of herself, himself, theirselves... It means that we are able to bring our entire selves into the movement... It means a holistic approach."

ANGELA DAVIS ON RADICAL SELF CARE

Most entrepreneurs are very passionate about their business mission, but their personal health falls victim to neglect while they're grinding for professional success. They feel there's no time for self-care, and it's not worth the investment. However, the benefits of self-care are priceless.

Feel like you are struggling to stay afloat?

Competition is among the top five reasons so many small businesses fail, according to Forbes (www.Forbes.com). It's no surprise that your palms sweat, your heart runs like a marathon, and your head throbs from the pressure after you make that final stroke on your keyboard to send your proposal via email. It feels like torture as you anxiously suffer in silence, waiting to hear from your prospect... praying that they will accept it. A rejection may even send you into depression. This is why business owners must make self-care a priority.

Self-Care Mastery is a Must to Avoid Your Business Lights Burning Out

I understand that you may wear all the hats, and it seems impossible to put aside your strategic business plan to focus on *soft skills*. Nonetheless, you cannot run a business with your mental health tank on "empty." You started out on fire with your new business. You were excited and ready to make a huge impact to possibly millions.

Then, your enthusiasm fizzled, and your business plan that you worked so hard on starts hiding further and further underneath that stack of unpaid bills and miscellaneous papers on your desk. You cannot figure out what happened.

You want to make a difference but are stuck. You feel numb. Eventually, you give up. That's unfortunate. Why? Because only you can fulfill the Divine business assignment that God has given you.

But it's not too late…

It's just time to recognize that you are three parts of a whole; mind, body, and spirit. Disruption to one part causes chaos in the others.
Simone Biles, the most decorated American gymnast, served as a true champion of putting "mental health first" when she bowed out of the Olympics in Tokyo.

Triple A Puts Your Self-Care First:

1. **Acknowledge** the signs. These can include stress, triggers, and bad habits that you are starting to adopt.
2. **Act now**. Create affirmations of success and healthy boundaries, and schedule psychotherapy appointments.
3. **Automate self-care** in your daily routine, just like your marketing plan in business. Don't wait until a crisis.

How much bigger an impact can you make with self-care mastery?

Wealth has no limits once your inner work begins. Balance in work, life, and relationships is achievable.

When you neglect self-care, terrible things can happen, such as instability and a bad case of imposture syndrome. Not fit to serve at your fullest potential, you won't make the kind of impact you desire.

Imagine being mentally healthy, your business thriving, and not worrying about the competition. Your clients will surely be in good hands.

To receive my newsletter with more tools and strategies for personal and professional health, visit https://affinity411.com/

Montrella Cowan, LICSW

Crushing barriers to mental health and wellness, Montrella Cowan is a licensed therapist, life coach, speaker, and CEO. At her company, Affinity Health Affairs, LLC, she supports women, men, and children by providing a clear roadmap from darkness and distress into the light of healing and happiness.

If you're ready to smash the past, co-create your future, and unleash your undeniable impact, Montrella can show you how. Visit her at Affinity411.com.

Let's stay connected:
IG: @Affinity411
FB: @MAffinity411

Inspirational Message by
Karwanna D.

"Live Life by Design, Not by Default"
KARWANNA D.

For those who have dreams deferred, know that it's never too late to re-ignite those dreams. The greatest gift I've discovered in life was my ability to speak things into existence even when everything around me made it appear impossible.

Growing up in the hood, in a single-family home to a mother of 7, all I knew was struggle. Watching my mother work hard to provide for us taught me the value of hard work. I had a great childhood despite being poor, but in my mind, I knew I didn't want to inherit the same paycheck-to-paycheck lifestyle, barely making ends meet.

So I aspired to, one day, own my own business. I had no idea how I was going to make that happen. Especially when in school, I was taught that I first had to struggle to be successful in business. I was told that I had to build my business on a shoestring budget, get loans that I may never be able to pay off, and basically go into debt with hopes that I would one day find my way out and hopefully make a profit. I don't know about you, but that didn't sound too promising to me.

In fact, I failed tremendously trying to follow those misconceptions that many of us are still being told to this day. When you add to that bad credit and denials for start-up loans, then it's no wonder so many small business owners never even get their business off the ground, and so we settle. Then one day, that big dream you once had suddenly becomes a distant memory.

This is exactly what happened to me until I discovered the #1 biggest kept secret that nobody shares and you would never even learn in business school. I coin it the Trillion Dollar Secret to Government Contracts. This was the secret that nearly every successful and thriving business knew but didn't share. This awakening came at a time when I was hopeless. I was struggling to make ends meet, in the middle of a divorce, living paycheck to paycheck and repeating everything that I once told myself I didn't want to repeat. And to top it off, the person I was divorcing intentionally left me high and dry with no intentions of even providing for his own children. Do you know what it's like as a parent to watch your kids walk around with clothes they've recently outgrown and shoes that were worn to the ground?

That's what re-ignited my dreams. All I had was a business license and motivation. That's when I took a serious look at this big kept secret called government contracts for small businesses and intended to learn everything I needed to learn to succeed in that endeavor. With this knowledge, I went from barely making ends meet on $20,000/yr to landing my first government contract as a small business that was $70,000 for just 28 days of work and went on to land multiple contracts simultaneously and now my mission is to teach everybody I know about it.

About dreams deferred... If you speak it, you can live it, but you must take action to make it happen. Don't just live life reacting to everything that happens, but remember to live life purposefully by design and know that it's never too late to re-ignite your dreams. I did, and so can you.

Inspirational Message by
Catrina Davidson

"Be strong and of good courage, do not fear nor be afraid of them; for the LORD your God, He is the One who goes with you."

DEUTERONOMY 31:6

The lights are on, and the glare from the audience is intense and palpable. It's go time, and everyone is waiting to hear what you have to say. It takes courage to endeavor to communicate. It takes fortitude to be determined to convey your ideas or philosophy through speech. It takes even more courage to think that you can do it effectively. After all, that is what effective communication is the ability to take our private ideas and clearly convey them to an impending, waiting audience.

The stress, tension, and trepidation seem overwhelming during the process of execution. Anxiety controls our minds with such thoughts as, "How do I sound? How do I look? Did they get it? Was it passionate? Was it polarizing? Did I talk too much? Did I say the wrong thing? Oh! I forgot to say that!" To stand in front of an audience and face this kind of scrutiny, no doubt, takes courage. Courage may be your greatest asset. Courage allows you to galvanize all you have studied, deny the gaze of potential outcomes and simply deliver, with grace, the message you intended. Having the courage to proclaim your message publicly can enhance or compensate you for your public speaking skills, ensuring the trajectory of the message that is intended hits your target. Most importantly, courage eradicates FEAR.

Are you aware that studies show that fear of public speaking is the number one fear people have?

That means that almost everyone we know has a fear of speaking publicly! Having courage will allow you to tear through the veil of self-inadequacy and find your true inner courageous self. Courage allows you to know that it is not in how eloquently the words were presented but in the fact you had the courage to convey them.

Our foundational scripture speaks of Joshua and the courage he needed as he had to make his first public address after a paradigm-shifting leader. To speak after Moses was literally like speaking after God himself. Joshua would have to find the right words. However, he found that the power was not just in his words but in his presence. He had to know and understand three key points:

1. God was presently with him in the moment.
2. He had to completely surrender to the voice of God and be present in the moment.
3. Joshua had to believe in the cathartic power and potency of the message he was presenting.

You see, true courage is derived from fully believing in what you have to say. The message you deliver may not even be popular or fun, but with courage and conviction, it can take on a new potency. Doing anything great requires having a courageous mindset. Courage does not mean being unafraid. It simply means that despite your fears, you will choose to "do it anyway." What you will find is that you have the exact thing that someone, or even a few somebodies, need!

Catrina Davidson

Catrina A. Davidson was born in Las Vegas, Nevada. At a young age, Catrina learned the importance of salvation, morals, self-worth and received Christ as her personal savior. At six years old, Catrina had her first appearance on a local radio broadcast, and soon after, more opportunities followed.

In 2002, Catrina met her husband, and to this union three beautiful children were born. Consistently striving for more, in 2008 Catrina successfully completed the Leaders of Righteous Dedication course and received her certification as a Leader in her Church.

Hard work and dedication are not foreign to her. With over 1000 Awards, Catrina is the first African American Woman to be awarded the title Grand Podium Ambassador in the Vacation Ownership Industry. Her unique style and poise impact the lives of everyone she meets. Catrina is the Founder and CEO of SPEAK Academy. Her voice is being heard around the world.

Inspirational Message by
Dr. Nakita Davis

"....You Will Win"

JEKALYN CARR

Growing up as a little girl, I always knew that I would do Great things!

Despite my environment and long before I knew about the saving Grace and Mercy of King Jesus, my mother, God rest her soul, told me that *I Could Do and Be ANYTHING!*

I Believed her, and So I Did.

Like many tales from the hood, my upbringing wasn't the prettiest picture. My mother and stepfather both worked 2 and 3 jobs at times just to put food on the table. We stayed in the hood. Violence in the neighborhood, random gunshots at night, fish fry's on Fridays, and everybody running to the mailbox on the 1st and the 15th, hoping to get a government check.

In those days, my mother and Stepfather showed my sister and me the real value of a dollar and instilled the ferocious work ethic and love for the Lord that I have today.

One of my fondest moments was in the 8th grade. I always loved to read and write. I was the classroom poet and very outspoken. One day my teacher told me about an opportunity for a program called *Love of Learning*. This highly selective program would allow me, if chosen, a free summer internship at Davidson College. All I needed to do was write an essay along with some other scholarly requirements. I excelled in school and sports, so this was no concern. I aspired to attend Duke University.

I submitted my essay, and to my surprise, I made the final cut. I was ecstatic, but the final decision required an in-person interview with the program Dean.

My heart sunk

Not because I didn't think I would do well but because my family didn't even have a car. My parents walked 1 to 2 blocks to catch the bus for work. Add in snow this winter, and I could kiss my internship dreams goodbye.

Fast-forward

My Mother, after scrubbing floors and cleaning toilets at work, still found someone to give us a ride in the snow to Davidson College so that I could be interviewed.

Be Encouraged

- *We didn't have a car when I was in the 8th grade, but God still provided a way for my interview, and I Nailed the Internship at Davidson College!*
- *I never went to Duke University, but I still became Dr. Nakita Davis - Glory to God!*
- *I didn't become a Blue Devil (Duke mascot), but Now I get to CRUSH the Devil under MY FEET EVERYWHERE I GO! As an Ordained Minister helping raise God's daughters up in the Marketplace, Authorship, and so much More!*

- *That Little Girl Who had a **Love for Learning** now Inspires, teaches, and equips Women Across the WORLD to do the same!*

MY FRIEND, TAKE GOOD CHEER!
IT'S NEVER TOO LATE!
IT DOESN'T MATTER WHAT IT LOOKS LIKE!
IF GOD BE FOR YOU!
HELL, AND HIGH WATER CAN COME AGAINST YOU!
BUT BABY - IN JESUS NAME - YOU STILL GONNA WIN!

IF ONLY YOU BELIEVE!

SO, BELIEVE, WIN BIG, and GO DO GREAT THINGS FOR HIS GLORY!

Dr. Nakita Davis

Dr. Nakita Davis is a #JesusGirl! She is an Award-Winning Powerhouse Speaker, 10x Best-Selling Author, and Multiple 6 Figure Girlboss. She is the Proud CEO and Founder of Jesus, Coffee, and Prayer Christian Publishing House LLC; the Owner of the Women Win Television NETWORK and Digital Magazine. Her Juggernaut publishing, speaker, media, and PR platforms position Women to SOAR across the globe! Her team has Sponsored the Stellar Awards, PR campaigns for both Grammy and Superbowl Billboards, in addition to working with highly driven Queens from around the globe. (As Seen On ABC, NBC, CBS, and FOX)

Dr. Davis has garnered support from Dorinda Clark-Cole, JeKalyn Carr, Coko (SWV), BRAVOs-Dr. Heavenly Kimes and is affectionately known as the Billboard Queen and Atlanta Book Hitmaker. She is an Official For(bes) the Culture Member and resides in Atlanta, GA, with her loving husband and two children.

Stay connected with this Trailblazer:
IG @jesuscoffeeandprayer and @womenwinnetwork
Learn More: www.jesuscoffeeandprayer.com

Anissa Green Dotson

"Pursue your Purpose with Passion because your current circumstance does NOT dictate your future!"

ANISSA GREEN DOTSON

John Ortberg says, "If you want to walk on water, you've got to get out of the boat!" That is a quest many entrepreneurs face every day when seeking guidance and clarity on their new ideas, wondering if their product or service will be successful. The truth is, analysis paralysis is very real, and in life, you are destined to miss *all* of the shots you never take by overthinking or worrying how your dreams will come to pass. God requires us to do the daily work and have faith in Him, and He will align the right people in our path with the right connections in His precise timing. Here are four tips to help you take that leap of faith and move forward despite your doubts and fears. You must get M.A.D.D.! (Meditation, Affirmations, Discipline, and Determination.)

Early rising is essential to quiet the noise in your head and your surroundings. When you awake and begin your morning Meditation with an attitude of gratitude, it ignites your brain to prepare for something great. In conjunction with your morning Meditation, speak and listen to your daily Affirmations. What do you want? Why are you pursuing God for this? What is the reason behind the madness entrepreneurs contend with – late hours, sleep deficiency, thoughts and ideas downloading while showering, and friends or family members staring at you in disbelief while sharing your goals with them?

Life handed me a set of uppercuts after my daughter, and I lost everything we owned in the 2001 Allison flood. Afterward, I went through a tumultuous divorce, my Fortune 500 employer went bankrupt, and my body broke down, leading to hospitalization. But God! No time to give up; my daughter needed me. If I was ever going to walk again, it was time to call on a higher power. The Discipline to stand up daily in the midst of my pain, placing one foot in front of the other, taking one step at a time, was not easy. But my daughter needed me. Prayers, strength, and Determination helped me to get up and get going.

It's imperative when life slaps you (and life will slap you) that you fight thru those temporary distractions, silence the enemy, and stay focused! Be very intentional when you begin each day. Stop watching the morning news, monitor your words daily, and speak only the results you seek; never speak about the current situation. Head high and shoulders back, congratulations - you have just gone thru hell and survived! I'm sure you wanted to quit dozens of times. However, your story was not just for you. It is to give back. Reach back and Bless someone else.

On your journey to success, remember how powerful you are! Your message must be heard, and the world needs your products or services. Practice getting M.A.D.D. and watch the manifestations in your life. You have been equipped, so now go out and DOMINATE your day!

Anissa Green Dotson

Anissa Green Dotson is a Speaker, Money Motivator, Best-Selling Author of *"DOMINATE! 7 Steps to Success for Single Moms,"* Owner of Dotson Development & Construction, and Founder of Single Moms United Organization. She challenges women all over the globe to "Pursue your Purpose with Passion because your current circumstance does not dictate your future." Anissa's vision to teach life skills and empower women to succeed was a direct result of her homelessness in 2001.

Anissa is a loving wife to Mike, and they share a blended family of 5 with "Max the mischievous puppy." She's an avid reader, enjoys the beach, and loves listening to birds. As a philanthropic teacher, she constantly seeks ways to bless others and asks, "Have you blessed someone today?" Anissa asserts you should strive daily to Exceed Expectations, then go out and DOMINATE™ your day!

Please visit www.dotsondominates.com to learn more about me!

Inspirational Message by
Monique Carkum Edwards, Esq.

"You don't get what you deserve. You get what you fight for, and you'll end up with whatever you settle for. So knuckle up and guard your grill."

MONIQUE CARKUM EDWARDS, ESQ.

While speaking to a crowd, Jesus said in John 10:10, "The thief's purpose is to steal and kill and destroy. My purpose is to give them a rich and satisfying life." Jesus came to give us a life full of purpose, brimming with vitality and overflowing with impact - anything but mediocre. Your John 10:10 preferred life will use your unique God-given gifts in a way that leaves a unique, unforgettable impact now and throughout eternity. Yeah, fam, it's that big!

But John 10:10 also says the thief comes not to give life but to steal, kill and destroy it. This thief, the enemy of your soul Satan, will stop at nothing to keep you from experiencing that rich and satisfying life. Are you really going to let him run up on you and steal your God-ordained purpose, vitality, and impact? Every time you sit on your gift, play small, and procrastinate on your calling, you're letting the devil jack your purpose, provision, and peace. It's time for you to snatch back what that joker has stolen from you. Imagine refusing to settle for anything less than that rich and satisfying John 10:10 life. Think about the people you'd impact as you fulfill the purpose God has for you. It's time for *Operation Snatch Back.*

If you're ready for that John 10:10 life, you need to identify and break unhealthy norms in three critical life domains: the *thoughts* you entertain, how you invest your *time,* and who you *trust* so you can live the preferred, rich and satisfying life God planned. Through *Operation Snatch Back*, you're going to *thrive, not merely survive.*

This isn't called "Operation Pretty Please Can I Have It Back?" - the enemy of your soul isn't going to back down because you used your polite words. The enemy wants to steal your purpose, kill your vitality, and destroy your impact. He didn't come to play. So neither should you. The word *snatch* means to quickly seize something in a rude or eager way. Don't get it twisted: you will have to *forcibly* take back your thoughts, your time, and your trust from things that are robbing you. This is no time to be polite. When it comes to obtaining your John 10:10 life, you're in a fight with the enemy of your soul. And I've never seen a polite fight. So stop clutching your pearls - knuckle up and reclaim your preferred life from the clutches of mediocrity.

It's time you take a good hard look at some ingrained thought patterns and reclaim your mind from stinkin' thinkin'. Start cherishing the time God has given you here on earth and take back control in order to maximize it. Call out the stumbling blocks that keep you from trusting God, others, and yourself, and live free of fear and uncertainty. A rich, satisfying and impactful future is waiting for you. It's time for Operation Snatch Back. Let's go!

Monique Carkum Edwards, Esq.

She's an attorney, entrepreneur, author, pastor, wife, and mother, but above all, Monique's a woman born to unleash greatness in others. Through Gravitas Executive Consulting, Monique helps professional people of faith amplify their impact through leadership development, strategic visibility, and spiritual renewal.

Described by her clients as dynamic and results-focused, Monique has coached countless executives at FaceBook, NBC Universal, Microsoft, Delta Airlines, Morgan Stanley, and many other companies. Monique is also a Chair with The C12 Group, helping C-Suite executives solve their most pressing business problems. Prior to Gravitas, Monique spent 20 years as a corporate attorney for the Fortune 50. After retiring from law, she served as the executive pastor for a growing local church.

Monique's book "The Snatch Back" is a clarion call for boldly reclaiming your life from the lies that have stolen your purpose, vitality, and impact. Let's connect at www.moniquecarkumedwards.com.

Inspirational Message by
Tonya Fairley

"When one door of happiness closes, another opens, but often we look so long at the closed door that we do not see the one which has opened for us."

HELEN KELLER

Being raised by a drug-addicted mother and absent father would lead one to believe that my life was destined to fail. Experiencing physical and mental abuse at the hands of the one who gave you "physical life" would lead one to believe that I would remain in an angry and bitter state. Being placed in a foster home would further lead one to believe that a life as such is worthless and not worthy of that "agape" kind of love. I learned early on that one's perception is another person's reality, and because of this thought, I knew my life was far from worthless but worthy of all God had planned for me.

At a young age, I knew the hand I was dealt was not the end story. At the hands of my birth mother, I experienced a beating as if I was a stranger she met in the alley. I was left bloody on the floor with a busted eardrum, a burn from the beating with an extension cord on my left thigh, and made to lay in soiled clothing until she fell asleep. That night I prayed to God and asked Him to save me before she killed me. The following day I went to school, and my life changed forever. My brother and I were placed in a transition space for foster kids as we awaited our fate. I had no regrets. It was as if God said Himself, "peace be still, my child, trust the process." Scared and afraid of my new surroundings, I felt a sense of peace and comfort that I could go to sleep and not worry about if I would have another meal or how angry she would be that day. This was the turn of a new beginning for me, and all I had to rely on was my foundation of God and the teachings from Sunday school. I knew the Bible said, "God would not give you more than you could bare" but at the age of 12, I had no true understanding of this. All I knew at that moment was again, I was abandoned, first by my father, second by the woman who gave me birth, and third by the family that should have saved me. I knew at that moment I needed to see myself better than the world was about to see me, or else I could repeat this same cycle when I got older. It only took a person or two to remind me that I was worthy of being loved and smart enough to see the change God was making in me despite my circumstances. After all, life threw at me, who would have thought I would have a family and build several 6 figure businesses? I am reminded that each journey is a chapter in a book and not the end of the story. I decide where to put the period!

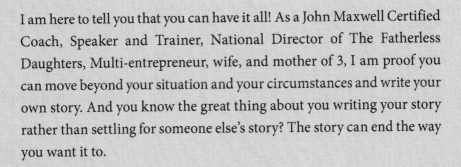

Tonya Fairley

Tonya Fairley CEO/Founder of Root
Success Coaching, Strandz Unlimited,
Strandz Hair Studio, and Strandz Unlimited
Beauty Supply.

I am here to tell you that you can have it all! As a John Maxwell Certified
Coach, Speaker and Trainer, National Director of The Fatherless
Daughters, Multi-entrepreneur, wife, and mother of 3, I am proof you
can move beyond your situation and your circumstances and write your
own story. And you know the great thing about you writing your story
rather than settling for someone else's story? The story can end the way
you want it to.

Find out more at www.tonyafairley.com

Inspirational Message by
Dr. Monique Flemings

"The Human Voice is the most perfect instrument of all."

ARVO PÄRT

"You sound like you just got off a bus from the country." These words rang out from my high school English teacher just after I finished my speech in a public speaking class. As an impressionable young lady, I admired my high school teachers. They were the epitome of black excellence. Many of them had graduated from prestigious HBCU - Historical Black Colleges and Universities, and they brought a depth of richness and pride to the classroom. To walk through the halls and see these pillars of educated black men and women allowed me to set my bar in life high. The sky was the limit. They were my walking heroes.

Words are powerful, and words were able to inflict pain. When this statement was made by my High School English teacher, it came to crush my authenticity at the core.

Here's how I embraced my sound!

I am not responsible for the opinions of others. What was spoken was that teacher's opinion and not the truth about me. People can say many things about you, even people of influence. That is their opinion, and their opinion does not mean that it is the truth. This was difficult because I wanted people's opinions of me to line up with the truth about me and the two are not the same.

Freedom began when I recognized the two are not the same, and I am not responsible for the opinions of others. Additionally, I cannot be attached to what others think about me because I will always try to live my life according to their standards. This teacher was an English teacher, but she was not the captain of my destiny. She was not the person that would open the door to my next step in life. I fumbled a lot in life because I searched for the opinions of others to be my truth. **The truth of who I am is not at the opinion of others**.

My "sound" was my gift from God. It was my swag, and it was how He created me. It was how He was going to use me to carry out my assignment. To be anything other than what HE created would be a slap in the face of God, my creator. How dare I tell God that He made a mistake in crafting me based upon the opinion of someone that had not created me.

Today decide that your voice, your sound will not be muzzled. You have a uniquely incredible sound that will allow you to reach a specific set of people. You were born great. Do not allow the opinions of others or even the negative opinion of yourself to stop you from using your voice.

Today decide to speak to bring healing to others. Speak to set the captives free. Speak and change lives. Yes, it is time to unleash your undeniable sound.....the world is waiting on your voice!! The world is waiting on your sound!

Dr. Monique Flemings

With over three decades of leadership, healthcare, and ministry experience, Dr. Monique Flemings uses her diverse background to transform lives. A builder of people, as the CEO of Monique Flemings Enterprises, she unmuzzles women to walk in their authenticity through digital education, coaching, and anthology projects. She is a proven solutionist for people in a transition and is affectionately called The Transitions Dr.

As the CEO of A Safe Place Consulting, where the total health of leaders is addressed through burnout prevention strategies, Dr. Monique counsels leaders of various diverse backgrounds into wholeness. An unapologetic apostolic voice for this generation, she serves as the Director of Affiliate Churches for All Nations Collective, an urban church planting organization. A 12 x author, powerful preacher, and speaker, her practical yet thought-provoking style with a sprinkle of humor is transformational and healing all at the same time.

Website www.moniqueflemings.net, Email: dr.monique@monique-flemings.net

Inspirational Message by
Dr. Lisa Coney-Fonville

"This time next year, you're gonna
wish you had started today."

KAREN LAMB

As a mover and shaker, I wondered what I could have accomplished had I not stayed so long in the shadows and played it safe. Of all the encouragement and achievements I experienced in life, I was so reluctant to snap into place and go for the gusto. Needless to say, I missed so many opportunities playing it safe and put off making BOSS moves that could have launched me towards ultimate success. I often left money on the table because I thought I wasn't ready to launch my own business, become an author, or speak empowerment into the lives of others.

Let me share with all my ladies and gentlemen who will listen. There is so much within us that we were born with to make our lives and the lives of others something to write home about. I was once told that people would pay you $20 an hour to build their dreams and forget yours. My father, an extremely modest man, shared with me that my employer would NEVER pay me enough to purchase a home next to him/her. He encouraged me to use my creativity and my mind to create the life I deserve.

I want to encourage you to look for every opportunity in every situation that arises in your life. I would be lying if I told you I wasn't afraid to start my own business, pursue higher education, take a trip out of the country, and the list goes on. But I'm glad to report that I did it. I did it afraid when I launched my coaching business, I did it alone when I took challenging jobs, I did it with lint in my pocket when I invested in myself. I'd love to say "I came up," but the truth be told, "God came through."

There are so many miracles, advancements, and opportunities on the other side of your fear. Make your mark in the world and take advantage of opportunities presented to you. This means that you're going to have to rise above the noise, sidestep the naysayers, stretch beyond your limits, take risks and step forward into greatness.

You don't need anyone's permission to succeed. As God elevates you from whatever position you are in life, you'll notice the air will become cleaner, your circles will be more encouraging, your mindset will be elevated, and you will become empowered to conquer whatever goals you set for yourself. Just a reminder, set your goals beyond your limits, otherwise, they are not goals, they are just tasks.

Ladies and gentlemen, as you create your boundaries and get your balance, I encourage you to maximize on every opportunity possible. Don't delay on your life and goals. Respect your time. Once time is spent, you get no change back. If you have plans, get busy accomplishing them – remember – this time next year, you're gonna wish you had started today.

Dr. Lisa Coney-Fonville

Dr. Coney-Fonville is an influential speaker, an expert in self-esteem development, and a published author of her first inspirational work of love titled "Missed Opportunities." She is also an author, along with other Drs. in an anthology outlining their Ph.D. journey. She serves as a mentor with the Black Women Leaders in Nursing, Inc., and is the founder of E.L.I.T.E. Life Coaching (Empowered Life Inspired To Elevate). She inspires women to step outside their comfort zone and establish their goals towards a better life.

Dr. Coney-Fonville believes that developing a strong and positive relationship is the foundation of everything she does, both professionally and personally. She focuses her attention on supporting and encouraging women in balancing their family, work, and education. Dr. Coney-Fonville is focused and determined to make a positive impact and be influential in the lives of others.

Contact Dr. Coney-Fonville on IG, FG, Twitter, & LI

Inspirational Message by
Mimi Foxwell

"If my mind can conceive it, My heart can believe it,
I know I can achieve it!"

JESSE JACKSON

Hello, wonderful being! Welcome onboard the journey of self-discovery and fulfillment. First things first, the ticket for this journey is to give yourself permission to make the necessary stops for you to flow in your purpose. Please don't treat this as if it's an option because it is not. Your life depends on it. To fully open up and unleash, you must address why you are locked. Are you held back? Let go of things that don't serve your new, freed self.

Unleash:

Unleashing is a beautiful thing, revealing your true self, letting all your glory shine through like becoming a butterfly from a caterpillar. It may be uncomfortable or straight out frightening. But you got this! And when you do, the greatest rewards will follow. You can take that to the bank, and you will. Don't allow yourself to doubt it. You're not losing anything but gaining. Once you can fully conceive the vision, you can start living the vision.

Develop a way to carry it in your heart and never let it out of your spirit. Visualization is a process that will help. Start seeing yourself walking in your purpose. Now that's a beautiful sight. Start living and breathing that picture.

Next, you have to address who or what is your oppressor. I don't know if it's a person or a belief, but they are not bigger than your purpose. If it's a person, spend as little time as possible with them. If it's YOU, develop a new mindset, one that will carry you to the next level. Start by reading several inspirational books. But don't stop with just reading. Pick a strategy and implement it in your daily activity. Let that inspirational message be your mantra and a shield when you need it.

Undeniable:

What belongs to you? Just to you. Even in a room filled with people, you'd be the one that...? I hope that was easy for you to determine. Many people can't discern what sets them apart from others, the special characteristic that belongs to them. We all have something that is God-given. It is placed with you even before your birth certificate. This birthright is almost like a birthmark, given so that every person has a special gift that will help them succeed in life. And nobody can take it from you. Use it. It's your credit card that has no limit.

Impact:

We are here to make a difference on this planet. And there's no better way than with a great force. How do you view force? Some see it as something to avoid. But embracing it gets you farther. Riding a wave could push you at the Feet of Purpose faster and stronger.

You are a force of nature placed here to make a huge impact in the world. Unleash. The world is waiting.

Mimi Foxwell

Mimi Foxwell is a certified mediator and restorative justice facilitator who is on a soulful mission to help others have peace in their lives. As a coach and consultant, she brings a creative approach for women to uncover their true leadership potential and legacy. Mimi's BA in Psychology from Clark Atlanta University was only the start for her in the study of human behavior that includes a certification in positive psychology and applied neuroscience. As the founder of Conflict 2 Calm, she focuses on increasing emotional wellness. When not speaking or coaching on emotional intelligence, Mimi can be found pursuing her passion for crafting, increasing her wine expertise, and spending time with her family.

To connect with Mimi
Conflict2Calm.com
IG@ sisterintheroom

Inspirational Message by
Carol Campbell-Fullard

"Accept yourself, your strengths, your weaknesses, your truths, and know what tools you have to fulfill your purpose."

STEVE MARABOLI

Our journeys happen for a reason. It is through them we establish the possession of power. Unfortunately, many times we focus on the failures experienced during these transitions. We get trapped in imperfections that give influence to our insufficiencies. We remain unable to push past these temporary limitations to recognize they serve as an anchor for our breakthrough and greatest moments.

Stop getting stuck in behaviors that create continuous empty patterns. Stop being incarcerated and chained to a life you do not want. Stop living imprisoned by fear and self-imposed faults. Instead, create a vision and go after it. *Unleash Your Undeniable Impact.* Your power does not live on the hill in a White House nor in a private boardroom where "leaders" debate and dictate decisions. It lives in YOU! Every day commit to taking small, powerful steps to achieving your goals. Along the way, celebrate and embrace life. Live full out and enjoy the power that will be yielded from the journey!

Interruptions in life serve to shift your mindset. There may be cracks in the surface of your life that are caused by mounds of hurt and mountains of pain that swell and continuously bear down on you. However, now is the time to chisel through the anguish, dislodge hurt, and get unstuck. Take the time to confront the debris and grit in your life so that healing may occur as God intended. These interruptions have come to feverishly fuel and form your undeniable spirit! Amid these ill-conceived predicaments, remember that the power of possibilities exists. Embrace the interference of fear and anxiety. Let them provoke you to your next step. Now is the time to prepare your mind and plan.

Intention is the plan. At the root of each person's pain lies possibility. It is the driving passion that aligns us with our mission. According to Steve Maraboli, "Accept yourself, your strengths, your weaknesses, your truths, and know what tools you have to fulfill your purpose." This is the spirit of intention. It is disrupting all that mental chatter that does not serve your vision. Negate those "thinking traps" and begin to create a plan with objectives and strategies. Establish *SMART Goals* and recognize the benefits of achieving them. This is when the pursuit of purpose begins. "Write the vision and make *it* plain..." Habakkuk 2:2.

Impact is purpose in action. It is achieved when we move beyond preparation and plans. It is when we pivot and position ourselves to walk in a perceived purpose with action. Each day become accountable for the progression of outlined goals. Let this time flow so the collaborative journey of mindset and skill set can be in motion. This is when transformation occurs. God has given you a gift. When are you going to use it? Your story, your struggle, and your comeback has happened for a reason. It is time to influence the world through your I.M.P.A.C.T.

Intentionality
Mastery
Purpose
Action
Courage
Talent

Carol Campbell-Fullard

Carol Campbell-Fullard was born in London, England, to Jamaican parents who immigrated to New York City, where she grew up. She has served as an educator for over 20 years. Her experience has spanned from teaching in the classroom to being a middle school principal. Beyond the practical experiences garnered in public education, she is the CEO and Founder of I Am My Pieces LLC. Her company offers personal, professional, and leadership development coaching. She received her Bachelor's in Speech Communication from Ithaca College, Master's in Education from the City University of New York at Lehman College, and Executive Masters in Leadership from Georgetown University. She is co-author of the Amazon Best Selling book, Unmute Yourself. For coaching, professional development, and speaking services, reach out to carol@iammypieces.com or on Instagram @iammypieces. Her website is www.iammypieces.com.

Dr. Jonas Gadson, Known As "Mr. Enthusiastic!"

"You can have everything in life you want if you just help enough other people get what they want!"

ZIG ZIGLAR

There are three kinds of people: Those that make things happen! Those that watch things happen! And those that wondered, what happened?

I am a person that makes positive things happen, and I believe that you are too!

Say Yes To Your Success! I have learned that the only place you find success before work is in the dictionary. Success leaves steps. Bonus from Jonas, "There is no secret to success, but there is a system to success!"

Now I will spell out the word success in acrostics, where the first letter of each line spells success:

S See - Some people are blessed with 20-20 eyesight but have no vision. How do you see yourself and your future? Bonus from Jonas, "What you see is what you will be! If you want to be more, you must first see more!"

U You are Important. There are nearly 8 billion people on the planet, and there will never be another one just like you! Bonus from Jonas, "You were born an original! Don't you dare die a cheap copy!"

C Commitment – You must be committed to your dreams, your goals, and your aspirations! You must do the work because you are worth it! This is your time, and this is your turn! I invested $100,000 in my personal and professional development. Someone asked me, "Are you working hard to get somebody?" I said, "No. I am working hard to be somebody!" Bonus from Jonas, "Invest in the most important person on the planet, You!"

C Communication – Effective communication is the key to your success! It is the number one skill in achieving your goals. Whether you are giving a presentation to your board, making a sale, negotiating a contract, or interviewing for a new position, effective communication is critical. Bonus from Jonas, "If you cheat yourself in your preparation, it will show up in your presentation!"

E Education is a Latin word meaning "to lead and to draw out" the gift that is lying dormant in you! If you develop your gift within, you will never do without! Bonus From Jonas, "Opportunity may knock, but it will never pick your lock!"

S Stand - You must stand firm and fight for what is right and live the life you desire and deserve! You have learned that the sky is not the limit; your belief is! And that you can always "Better your Best!"

Bonus From Jonas
"When your value is clear, your decision is easy!"

Bonus From Jonas
"You cannot change your past, but you can change your path!"

S Service - I like what Dr. Martin Luther King Jr. said, "Everybody can be great because everybody can serve!" We need more leaders to pick up the towel and put down the title and serve humanity! I have learned that "service is the rent we must pay for the space we take up on this planet, and some of us are behind on our rent!"

Dr. Jonas Gadson

Dr. Jonas Gadson, DTM, known as "Mr. Enthusiastic!" is an International Motivational Speaker, Corporate Trainer, Radio Personality, Author, and Expert Communication Coach. He worked 30 years for two Fortune 500 companies, Xerox Corporation and Eastman Kodak Company. At Eastman Kodak, he trained over 8,000 employees from 69 countries and earned the Trainer of the Year Award. He is a Distinguished Toastmaster, a graduate of Dale Carnegie, and has a Doctorate Degree in Theology. He was inducted into the Beaufort High School Alumni Hall of Fame for distinguishing himself in profession, leadership, and service! He is the author of "How To Fly Like An Eagle With Wings Like A Wimp!" and has a chapter in three books; "Make It Matter!" "I Am A Victor!" And "You Are Enough!" His Motto Is: "Since Greatness Is Possible Excellence Is Not Enough! Go For Greatness!"

jg@jonasbonus.com. (585) 703-9547. Get your FREE Gift when you go to: www.jonasbonus.com.

Inspirational Message by
T. Renee Garner

"...Truly, truly, I say to you, whoever believes in me will also do the works that I do; and greater works than these will he do because I am going to the Father."

JOHN 14:12

The Greater Works! YOUR better version of yourself. Scripture says if you abide in Jesus and His words abide in you, you can ask anything, and Jesus will do it. Releasing your undeniable impact plays an important role in the world. Essentially you are understanding your purpose so that you may, in return, impact those you meet. Essentially you are willing to unleash your Greater Works!

Let's face it, life can and will be rough. Everything around you looks and feels exhausting. What do you do when your undeniable impact is so negative that, if unleashed, it will impact in an unpleasant way?

It is absolutely simple looking from my 20/20 view lenses now! You become YOUR better version of yourself.

How do you become your better version of yourself? Where is the starting point? Scripture says in John 10:27-28, "My sheep hear my voice and I know them and they follow me and I give unto them eternal life and they shall never perish neither shall any man pluck them out of my hand."

Let's start with just the first part of the scripture. "My sheep hear my voice." Your starting point is to become a sheep that a shepherd goes off to find. Learn from the voice of God and measure your negative past.

Here are four key takeaways for you to implement in releasing and moving forward to unleashing your undeniable impact.

LEARNED pinpoint in yourself to develop new behavior patterns. These are your learned behaviors. Write them down and measure them against your new way of thinking to release your undeniable positive impact.

Angels in Prayer be ambitious. Wayne Dyer says, "You are important enough to ask, and you are blessed enough to receive back." The ticket here is to be protective over your prayers and the answers.

Manage your Emotional Intelligence (EI). Understand the adversary, which is the enemy, is seeking how he can keep you stuck. A healthy response and a wise mindset are key towards problem-solving in LOVE.

Born Again is the key to Balance. Believe in the Lord God Almighty to make daily changes to unleashing your impact. Be true to God and love yourself. Romans 10:9-10 will become your Best Friend. It is Okay for you to Say it, Know It and Live It.
… "That if thou shalt confess with thy mouth the Lord Jesus, and shalt believe in thine heart that God hath raised him from the dead, thou shalt be saved.
For with the heart man believeth unto righteousness; and with the mouth confession is made unto salvation." Romans 10:9-10 KJV

T. Renee Garner

T. Renee Garner, Evangelist, is the owner of Inspiring Generations LLC, a production agency that brings your story to life through speaking, stage play performance, and short movie productions. T. Renee tells stories in a way that provides solutions to the audience using all the sensory parts of learning. T Renee is an activist who works tirelessly to bring awareness to domestic violence by telling her incredible story. She is a domestic violence and coma survivor. She is the founder of Inspiring Generation Enterprise, a nonprofit developed to bring awareness to the fight. The performance also includes components of consulting services, speaking, books, and other souvenir and keepsake products.

"...LOVE is patient, love is kind. It does not envy, it does not boast, it is not proud. It does not dishonor others; it is not self-seeking, it is not easily angered, it keeps no record of wrongs. Love does not delight in evil but rejoices with the truth. It always protects, always trusts, always hopes, always perseveres." 1 Corinthians 13:4-7

Speaking/Bookings: www.treneeinspires.com
Social Media: IG@treneegarner, Support: www.trenee.org

Inspirational Message by
Pamela R. Garrison

"If you are always trying to be normal, you will
never know how amazing you can be."

MAYA ANGELOU

*Y*ou are a unique, gifted treasure loaded with gems and jewels waiting for discovery. Life holds the key as tests and trials teach lessons that bring forth revelation. The journey sometimes seems lengthy, but I assure you, it is only for a season.

There was a time in my life when my days were filled with chronic pain—every part of my being hurt continually without relief. Imagine the pain of a toothache where the nerve is exposed, and you just bit down on it. Then imagine that the pain radiates throughout your body combined with equally excruciating muscle pain, and just when the pain is about to ease up, someone taps you on your shoulder, and it elevates all over again! I had no peace of mind and no foreseeable solution. Clearly my value of life had plummeted in the wrong direction. I was seen by multiple doctors and even reviewed excruciatingly by a whole student body at Stanford Medical Center in Palo Alto, CA. Every move I made only resulted in increased pain. My prognosis indicated that I would eventually lose the use of my limbs, spend the rest of my life in chronic pain, and be wheelchair-bound. I was certified disabled and left with no hope for a cure, according to medical staff.

Nothing about this report was normal. I had just turned 30 years old, and this had become my life's journey for a long season of 12 years. Even though I heard and read the medical reports, I refused to accept the projected outcome. My vision held a different destiny as I laid on my back, wondering what had I done so wrong and how was I coming out of this agony.

My healing was a process that involved a major adjustment of my mindset to see possibilities of a different outcome. Allow me to further share two key components that are essential to a victorious outcome.

Key #1 Stop Voicing The Problem

I remember someone asking me, "How was I doing?" My immediate response was to tell them all about my pain and misery until one day, I got a revelation. I realized that the pain was controlling me and consuming every area of my life. At this moment, I had a divine encounter where that quiet voice said to me, "You talk about that pain more than you talk about me. You esteem it higher than me." From that day forward, I made a strong decision not to speak of it again regardless of how much it hurts. My faith confession became "All is well."

Key # 2 Expand Your Vision

When your body is in constant pain and agony, focusing is not an easy task. However, you have to find a way to envision yourself in places and doing things that you desire to manifest with a constant expectation.
I am living my dreams. I hope that my story inspires you to unleash your undeniable impact!

Pamela R. Garrison

Pamela R. Garrison currently resides in Modesto, California, and is using her wheelhouse of wisdom and knowledge as CEO/ Founder of *BuBBles For Life*, a business dedicated to being instrumental in integrating solutions for change in the core areas of life.

Pamela R. Garrison is a woman of integrity, power, influence, and joy, illuminating minds while impacting lives. She is often described as insightful, energetic, trustworthy, witty, and bubbly.

Pamela R. Garrison is an International Bestselling Author of multiple books; Dynamic Speaker; Personal Development Strategist; Online TV and Podcast Personality; and Voiceover Actress.

Pamela R. Garrison is the mother of 3 and caregiver to her youngest child. She plans to implement a non-profit organization called "Taja's House" to bring support, resources, and awareness to parents of children with autism.

For additional information, please visit www.pamelargarrison.com.

Inspirational Message by
Dr. Chere M. Goode

"When God sends it to you, he will see you through it."

DR. CHERE M. GOODE

When God puts an amazing idea and a plan in your mind and heart, there is no time for procrastination or second-guessing. I vividly recall the constant nudging I received to start my Make Me Over Wellness business smack dead in the middle of the pandemic. Family and friends thought I was crazy to want to take such a daring risk to start a new business with the uncertainty of the economy. However, I am a firm believer that God does not start a fire inside of us that He cannot fuel. With faith and an abundance mindset, I propelled forward and started my new business that has been flourishing since its birth.

Remember that when God gives you a vision or idea for greatness that it is just for you. God knows the beginning, middle, and end of all things. Consistency, determination, commitment, knowledge, and a plan are all required to be successful in business. There will be times when you want to quit but do not! Stay the course. Grind even harder. Reach out to reliable, experienced sources for guidance.

Be flexible. Do not be afraid to change up the way you do things. Do not be a know-it-all. We can all learn something new every day. Make changes that align with the times and according to your customer needs and wants. Talk to your clients and get to know their specific needs. What works today may not work tomorrow, so stay diverse with your skillset.

Be visible. Visibility is imperative. People cannot support what they do not know exists. Every chance you get, talk about your business, advertise your business, and promote your business. Be a walking billboard for your business. Represent your brand by the colors you wear. Openly display your logo. Be known by your logo.

Be resilient. There has never been a business owner that has not taken losses, disappointments, and even had doubts as to whether they should continue in the entrepreneurial journey or not. These are the times your faith and resilience will be tested. This is when you need to cling tight to other successful entrepreneurs for guidance, a word of encouragement, and even tips on how to push forward. Every entrepreneur should have a vault of inspirational materials to rely on to recharge their zeal and energy for their businesses.

Be Balanced. It is imperative that you maintain balance as a business owner. Most business owners take on multiple roles, and this can be taxing. Taking time for self-care and recharging will aid you in maintaining your resilience in your endeavors. Sleep, a healthy diet, regular exercise, and a work schedule will keep you balanced. The goal is to maintain total harmony and be whole mind, body, and spirit as you pursue your goals.

Dr. Chere M. Goode

Dr. Chere M. Goode is the Founder/CEO of Total Harmony Enterprises and Make Me Over Wellness. Goode has been a Licensed Practical Nurse for over 30 years and is Nationally Certified in Hospice and Palliative Care, an area she currently specializes in. Goode is an 8 x #1 Best Selling International Author, Speaker and Wellness Coach, and an American Heart & Stroke Association Ambassador/Spokesperson. Known as the RECHARGE Strategist, Goode teaches professional women strategies for self-care to recharge their Mental, Physical, and Emotional batteries for success in life and business through her 8 Recharge Pillars of Self-Care. Goodes's teachings also emphasize the importance of self-care to enrich ones' life.

Connect with me at:
Totalharmonyenterprises.com
Makemeoverwellness.com
Ig & LinkedIn: @cheremgoode
Fb: @Drcheremgoode"

Inspirational Message by
Mijiza Green

"The secret of change is to focus all of your energy
not on fighting the old but on building the new."

SOCRATES

To create change, you must manage areas of life and change your mindset. To change your mindset, you must change something you do every day. That's what I had to do as I embarked on a new chapter after losing my dad. I had to reflect on my life. I began to reflect on the idea of what I should be doing at this time in my life and what stopped me from doing it. I began to reflect on my purpose. It was clear that I had a voice, that I was a game-changer, that I could impact and that I could be the change the world needed, but I didn't think I was qualified for such a task. After spending much of my energy fighting what I couldn't control, fighting the old way it used to be, and fighting battles that were not mine, I found myself exhausted and filled with many emotions because I could not understand how my life had changed so drastically and why. It's true when you are sick and tired of being sick and tired, the only place to look is up. I looked up and began to pray. I had to ask for forgiveness. Not forgiveness for others but the ability to forgive myself. I had spent all these years trying to prove that I was not that 13-year-old who got pregnant. That I was worthy of being treated like a queen and that I was ENOUGH. I had to forgive myself to be open enough to reflect on my life, release all the negativity in my life and be empty enough to receive all that was for me. It wasn't easy, but I did.

After a time, prayer, and an investment in learning what self-care truly was, I finally said yes to God's plan for my life. Saying yes was not easy, but it was the best decision I ever made—no more fighting what was old but beginning to put all my energy into the new me and what ultimately can be the new you. It required me to manage my time, relationships, vision, and gifts, amongst others. Managing areas in my life that allowed me to grow mentally and spiritually was the decision that changed my life. I am enough and have always been enough. I might not have known it if my heart didn't break when I lost my dad. The brokenness I felt allowed God to be the potter He is to mold me and build me back up. The emptiness in me allowed room for the Holy Spirit to intervene in my life and flow through me like water. If He did it for me, He could do it for you. Being broken and empty manifests some of God's greatest work! And that's YOU.

Mijiza Green

Mijiza Green is the creator of The Wellness Purse, designed to help women and teens manage their lives and mental health through faith-based coaching, advocacy, and classes. She is also a program consultant and has helped develop customized programs such as Treasured Jewels Mentor Program, Young Men Empowered, and GRACE Empowerment that have Inspired, Educated, and Impacted many lives in surrounding areas through her nonprofit organization Planting Seeds Community Outreach. Mijiza is an impactful speaker, mentor, author, and coach who has dedicated her life to encouraging youth and young adults to become leaders by building character, confidence, and courage through her S.E.L.F. techniques. STOP, EVALUATE, LISTEN & FORGIVE. Mijiza is a God-fearing woman, married to Nathanal Green Jr., mother of 4 and nana to 2 grandchildren, and a graduate of Morgan State University majoring in Psychology. She can be reached at www.thewellnesspurse.com and the wellness purse on all social media platforms.

Inspirational Message by
Duania Hall

"You wanna fly, you got to give up the
shit that weighs you down."

TONI MORRISON

The power of human relationships is an underestimated component of success. Those you're connected to will play a part in your life that has the potential to move you to the next level or keep you from ever making a move. Additionally, allowing the wrong people to have all-access passes to your life will weigh you down mentally and emotionally. This shift in your well-being affects how you serve in this world. You can't afford the deficit of bad company!

Unfortunately, many people are taught that to be alone is a deficiency, but it can enhance your capacity for healing. Societal norms tend to encourage glorifying connections even when they're toxic. Being alone is an opportunity for a healthy interruption of these norms. Time alone allows you to increase self-awareness, self-love, and self-care, which helps restore the sanity lost from being in unhealthy relationships that keep you from reaching your full potential.

Whether it's a family member, friend, business or intimate partner, the connection with bad company deprives you of living a life of purpose and extends that deprivation to every person you're assigned to empower. Bad company includes individuals who don't respect you, motivate you, support you, propel you, lovingly redirect you, or celebrate you. Many good men and women are in relationships with the wrong people, destroying their lives. They've experienced fear, depression, and suicidal thoughts while pretending everything is okay. They're deteriorating day by day, bit by bit, thirsting for elevation because they know they are meant for more. They are living in the sunken place, trying to find the compass for their identity that was evident when the relationship started.

Perhaps you can relate to these individuals who had the pursuit of their purpose intercepted by connections with the wrong people. You don't have to subject yourself to this anymore! You can choose to release yourself from the suffocation of toxic relationships and unleash the impact you were undeniably chosen to make in this world. Start by repeating this simple prayer:

"God, shine Your light on anything that is not right in my relationships. Let Your wisdom and discernment flood the gates of my intellect so that I know how to remove these distractions and roadblocks. And help me to commit to using my gifts at the highest level so I can empower your people in extraordinary ways. In Jesus' name. Amen."

Please know that no one can do what you do in the way that God created you to do it. You are a necessary tool for the elevation of others. As you take time to evaluate all your relationships, consider the IMPACT:

Identify how your relationships are guiding you.
Muster up the courage to set boundaries in your relationships.
Pray for wisdom and discernment to disconnect from bad company.
Affirm God's dream for you daily.
Commit to the tough decisions.
Trust that God will bring you better because it's time for you to fly.

Duania Hall

Duania Hall is a motivational speaker, poet, and best-selling author. As a women's empowerment life coach, she guides women in rebuilding their lives after trauma. A background in social work, community relations, and surviving multiple traumas has equipped her to help hundreds of women navigate through the aftermath of their traumatic experiences. Duania is passionate about increasing awareness of the crossover effects of domestic violence and other trauma. Through facilitating workshops, she educates nonprofit and faith-based organizations on ways to better serve survivors. Duania believes that every survivor's life matters and they deserve to be supported while reclaiming their WHOLE identity. Her mission is to shift the mindset that under-values survivors and solicit more advocates. She is also dedicated to teaching women how to prioritize their well-being and live a WHOLE, blessed life. Connect with Duania on the following platforms:

https://www.duaniahall.com, IG: dh_motivating4life, https://www.facebook.com/duania.hall

Inspirational Message by
Cathy Harris

"A life is not important except in the
impact it has on other lives."

JACKIE ROBINSON

It is difficult to admit, but with billions of other humans on the planet, we are not all that significant. That, I believe, is the message conveyed by the quote. We are irrelevant and unimportant, with one notable exception. According to the quote, the only thing that matters is our impact on the lives of others. That is the closest we as humans can come to immortality. We are called to assist others in living a better life, improve their condition, assist them in believing in themselves, and assist them in accomplishing more than they imagined possible. This is how you unleash your undeniable impact in the world. That, after all, is what matters. Assistance to others is critical on a variety of levels. One of the most critical is the effect on the other person. Then there is the sense of accomplishment that comes with assisting others, which is a significant reason for many people to assist others. Those who have been helped frequently feel compelled to assist others. Why is helping others important? When you help others, you maximize your impact on the world. In our lives, we want to find meaning. Helping others and learning how to make an impact on others will help us find meaning in our own lives. It meets our most basic human need to feel valuable while also fulfilling the human need to impact. The best way to grow as a person is to help others. We set aside the belief that one person can make only a minimal impact in the world and see for ourselves that even the smallest acts of kindness can significantly change lives. At the same time, however, those who make a positive impact in the world do not only get fantastic results in their work, but they have a powerful and uplifting impact on how they live their lives, too. They have a sincere interest in helping others, and they project abundant energy and positivity to those around them. People who have a strong influence on others are hopeful for their growth. Are you an enthusiastic, soulful, central woman, who needs more, but you do not know yet fully what "more" is or how to unleash it? You have had enough of always keeping yourself small. You have had enough of being stuck. You are prepared to break through any obstacles and expand your aspirations. Consider for a moment what you would have to believe in order to want to help others more. If you lack motivation, the change will only last as long as you think about it. If you change your way of thinking, the effects can last a lifetime. Your purpose has impact! The key to accelerating your growth and deepening your impact in both your professional and personal life is to use your purpose to help others.

Cathy Harris

Cathy Harris is an International Motivational Speaker, 4x Best-Selling Author, Domestic Violence Expert, Philanthropist, Life and Business Coach. Cathy is passionate about helping people share their stories, fire their fear, and become free to walk in their purpose. She provides messages of hope, inspiration, humor and encourages people to find their voice and use life's stumbling blocks to rebuild their own lives. Cathy is the recipient of the Wavy TV Channel 10 Who Care Award, the ZETA Phi Beta Sorority, Inc. Finer Woman Award, Hampton Roads Gazeti Exemplar Award, and the Garden of Hope Unity Award from Gethsemane Community Fellowship Church, among others. Cathy's work has been featured on many television stations such as The Hampton Roads Show, Wavy TV 10, WVEC News Channel 13, WTKR News Channel 3, Virginia This Morning, the Dr. Oz Show, and other media outlets. Connect with her on social media @ thefireyourfearcoach.

Chari Twitty-Hawkins

"Your talent is God's gift to you. What you
do with it is your gift back to God."

LEO BUSCAGLIA

D o you know that God has an amazing purpose for you? A phenom-
enal, jaw-dropping purpose for each one of us? Well, He does! The
pains, struggles, and triumphs that you have gone through are for the
greater good.

God has a purpose for all of those, and it's to inspire people all over the
world. To inspire those who are going through those same struggles and
feel like they are alone—feeling like they just can't make it, like they
can't get through this.

Have you ever felt that way? Think about who that person was that inspired you. God wants you to be that person for someone else. But you
can't if you hold it in.

Sharing your story will help others. It will awaken the conqueror in
them and help them to keep going while inspiring you too. It will show
you that you indeed have a voice that matters and will give you the
courage to keep sharing that voice!

No more keeping those wins to yourself!

So, why is it so hard for some of us to share our stories or use our gifts? When you have a powerful gift inside you, it is the devil's job to stop you from sharing it with the world. He wants to stifle it. Believe me, I know.

There was a time when I didn't feel good enough. I felt like my thoughts and my voice did not matter. If you're like me and you're a mom, especially African-American moms, we have for generations seen our moms, grandmas, aunties push their wants, needs, and passions to the back burner. They sacrificed their own ambitions to take care of everyone else.

Their voices became smaller and smaller and more insignificant. But our voices matter! They always have!

I encourage you to think about what God has within you that you need to share with the world. What is it within you that you know would bless somebody? Something that would lift them up and let them know that they are not alone?

Write it down. RIGHT NOW. Don't wait.

Don't doubt yourself and stop doubting God. God has a unique voice within each one of us, including you.

It's time to change your mindset and belief in yourself and your voice! That starts with speaking it, speaking a different narrative over your life.

Start saying the opposite of those negative thoughts that you have been telling yourself or that others have been telling you. Write down those negative thoughts you struggle with, cross them out, and write the opposite.

*Start to say things such as MY VOICE MATTERS.
*People need my voice in this world.

*God created me with an amazing purpose and voice. It is my job to share it with the world!

Say these things over and over until they become your belief, and you start taking action and sharing your voice, your story. The world is waiting on you.

Chari Twitty-Hawkins

Chari Twitty-Hawkins is a self-care coach for moms, inspirational speaker, poet, best-selling author, and founder of ChariT's Inspirational Creations faith-based jewelry. She has made it her mission to inspire moms all over the world to make themselves a priority by rediscovering the woman within, practicing self-love and self-care so that she can live her unique God-given purpose while being an awesome mom too!

Chari provides coaching and speaking from a place of transparency and understanding with a touch of tough love that helped her to push past her struggles to where she is today! Chari is a praying mother and wife who resides in Pearland, Texas.

Contact Chari by email at info@cicinspireme.com or visit her website at www.cicinspireme.com. Connect with me on Instagram at @ cicinspireme.

Inspirational Message by
Ayana Henderson

"Tell your Story. Impact Lives. Change the World."
SIDNEY SWEETLY

You are undeniably valuable. Yes, you! You were born that way, and you will die that way, but the real question is will you live that way? Are you willing to show the world what value you, and only you, can bring to the table? Well, if you are thinking to yourself, I'm not exactly sure what kind of impact I have on the world, allow me to break that down with six ways you I.M.P.A.C.T. the world!

INFLUENCE: Who you are alone has the power to help others see things differently, move differently, and think differently. Influence is not based on likes, shares, or comments. It's your perspective, your lived experiences, and your vantage point that makes you influential. No one can do anything quite the way you do! Believe it!

MEANING: You can add definition, shape, depth, and visibility in a way that only *you* can. People need to hear your story, your triumph, your heart. Your sheep need YOUR voice. There are people out there specifically waiting for you!

POWER & PURPOSE: I discovered that we all share a universal purpose, but how we carry out that purpose is unique to how we are designed. That universal purpose is simple: to serve others. You have heard Dr. Cheryl Wood say this many times, "Your story is about you, but it ain't for you." The power within you drives the purpose given to you!

ACTION: How do you become influential with meaning, power, and purpose? I couldn't take consistent action until I embraced the natural and authentic me. I am a lover of learning and teaching. When I share, I teach with humility and humor. That's unique to me. I can show up as I am, and it's enough. What qualities do you possess that are natural and comfortable to you? How can you implement that into how you show up in the world?

COURAGE, CONFIDENCE, CAPACITY: Don't doubt yourself! Don't count yourself out. Others might, but don't you dare! Everything you need is within you. Don't believe me? Your passion, purpose, experiences, perspective, motivation, and natural gifts and talents all come from within! You truly do have the capacity to be great!

TRUTH: So, what's the truth? The truth is that you are already making an IMPACT. The truth is you are valuable. The truth is you were born to be great, and you have everything you need within you. The truth is you are undeniably YOU, and that's enough!

The world you change doesn't have to be done on a grand scale to be impactful. It can start with those in your home or office. It can be on a stage, in a living room, or virtually. To impact is to have an effect on the lives of others. Prayer is impactful. Art is impactful. A shoulder to lean on, an ear to listen, or a word of encouragement are all impactful.

Be encouraged. Be inspired. Be you. The world is ready!

Ayana Henderson

Ayana Henderson is a best-selling author, speaker, and Women's Empowerment Life coach. Through her work in the human resources field for over ten years, she has learned three things people, specifically women, desire most: the desire to find out who they are, what they want, and how to show up as their authentic selves unapologetically. Drawing from experience over the last two decades as a wife and mother, and as a trainer in personal and professional development, she now coaches women who have lost their sense of self through their own healing journey to become Warrior Women. Ayana believes that when women are equipped with the right tools and can clearly articulate who they are and what they value, they can change the world! When Ayana is not coaching, she enjoys cooking, dancing, and watching rom-coms! To learn more about Ayana or Warrior Womanhood, please visit www.thecapacitycoach.com.

Inspirational Message by
Kim Bullock-Hennix

"Stand in your royal power and command your presence
without permission or apology. Crown on."

KIM BULLOCK-HENNIX

You were divinely created with a special purpose to unleash your undeniable impact on the world. King or Queen, you have royal DNA flowing through your veins. You were *Birthed into Greatness.* When you look at the acronym for **B**irthed **I**nto **G**reatness, it spells B.I.G. There is nothing small about you, so you were chosen to show up powerfully. Our Heavenly Father teaches us in Jeremiah 1:5, "Before I formed you in the womb, I knew you, before you were born, I set you apart." To be set apart means to be distinguished… to be unique… to be rare … to be extraordinary. You were birthed with a distinct intention that only you can accomplish. How you choose to execute your purpose is solely in your hands. No one else can take your place – This assignment was designed exclusively for you. We must dare to be great, to make bold decisions in spite of fear. Trust in the promises from our Heavenly Father; your path is destined to win. Before you were formed in your mother's womb, God knew the plans that He had to prosper you and surround you with success. William Shakespeare said, "Some are born great, some achieve greatness, and some have greatness thrust upon them."

As we look over our childhood and reflect on the various people God has placed in our lives, we learn they were simply instruments to help guide us along the road He has prepared for us. To abundantly experience the complete inheritance Jesus purchased for us at the cross, we must first understand our *Royal Identity.* Your identity unlocks your inheritance. When we become fully aware of who we are and who our Heavenly Father is. This is when we begin to recognize we have access to a Royal Inheritance due to our birthright. God believes in us and has planned a marvelous inheritance once we take ownership and begin to believe in ourselves. It does not matter what age we may be. Regardless of how long we've been walking with Jesus, the reality of our identity in Christ is crucial to our spiritual elevation and earthly mission. When we study the Bible, God promises in 1 Peter 2:9 to articulate all believers as royal priests. "But you are chosen people, a royal priesthood, a holy nation, God's special possession, that you may declare the praises of him who called you out of darkness and into his wonderful light.

The role of the Royal Family is to support Queen Elizabeth in State and national duties, as well as bring out important work in public and charitable service. This helps to strengthen national unity and stability. We have the same role in supporting our Heavenly King by shining bright with courage and serving his people. Now is your time to reign supreme in all of you. As a Royal Heir, you are committed to excellence and refuse to deny or minimize your brilliance. You were Birthed into Greatness!

Kim Bullock-Hennix

Lifestyle and Abundance Coach Kim Bullock-Hennix is a highly requested, results-driven Abundance Mindset Expert, Royal Protocol Spiritual Teacher, Elite Award-Winning Author and Coach, Revolutionary Leader, Founder and Advocate for the Ambitious Women Movement.

She serves masses of entrepreneurial women and online influencers with strategic masterclasses and seminars to inspire them to show up powerfully as Queen in their business and personal life. Kim has her bachelor's degree in Communications and earned a master's degree in Entrepreneurial and Organization Leadership with an emphasis in Christian Ministry.

Awards:

Earned 2nd place in Las Vegas Entrepreneurs Magazine for Top 25 Author's January 2021
Awarded 3rd place in Las Vegas Entrepreneurs Magazine for Top 25 Life Coaches January 2021

Awarded Most Influential Woman April 2021 in Exposure Magazine
Honored as Top 50 Most Influential Women in VIP Global Magazine May 2021, ranking 18th place

Website
www.KimBullockHennix.com

Inspirational Message by
Carmen M. Herrera

"People of integrity and honesty not only practice
what they preach, they are what they preach."

DAVID A. BEDNAR

Here she comes, looking like she was born with a silver spoon in her mouth, always talking about this creating wealth stuff! How is she going to understand my situation? She's never been there! How is she going to talk to me about getting my financial house in order? She's never been there! She's never had to go through the things I've had to financially, or anything else for that matter! I'm not trying to talk to her about my situation and all the mistakes I've made. She won't get it!

Little do people know, I've been there, and I do get it. I was my first student. I haven't always been CarmenWealth the Wealthpreneur, who now truly understands what it means to "create wealth from the inside out." Even with all my degrees, licenses, appointments, titles, and access to information, I wasn't practicing what I preached. I was what you call young and dumb. Here I was telling others what they should be doing with their money and helping them invest for the future. But I wasn't following my own advice. I was in my twenties, making a boatload of money and living life to its fullest. By day, I was educating, advising, and investing other people's money. By night, I was spending mine, all mine. What a hypocrite! It didn't take me long to figure out that God wasn't going to continue to bless my mess! Proverbs 13:11 says, "Easy come, easy go," and let me tell you, I got a good understanding of exactly what that means. I know the ramifications and what it feels like to spend more than you make, a foreclosed house and repossessed car later.

Look, I'd like to blame my behavior on the fact that I didn't have much growing up. Or that I wasn't taught how to be a good steward of my money. Or even go as far as blaming my misbehavior and bad choices on 400 years of slavery, Jim Crow, institutional racism, or economic disparities. Nope, I'm not going to go there. The truth is, some of that may have something to do with why African Americans in America as a whole are still dealing with a huge wealth gap. However, I'm going to keep it 100. That was not my story. Yes, I grew up in an impoverished neighborhood and was afraid to sleep at night because of the rat infestation in our home. No, I wasn't born with a silver spoon in my mouth. However, the bottom line is, I made bad financial choices early in my career that I'm not proud of. Back then, I didn't believe I deserved to be wealthy. Now, not only do I believe I deserve it, but that's what God wants for me so that I can continue to be a blessing to His kingdom. Thirty years ago, I was talking the talk but not walking the walk. Today, not only do I practice what I preach, I am what I preach.

Carmen M. Herrera

Carmen M. Herrera, award-winning Wealth Advisor, best-selling author, and speaker. She is the Managing Partner of CMHC Wealth Advisors, a leading wealth consulting firm.

Co-author of #1 best-selling book, Mission Unstoppable with Les Brown, and Dr. George C. Fraser. One of the country's most sought-after financial experts, Carmen has been featured by media outlets NBC, FOX, and more across the country. She toured the U.S. as a featured Financial Advisor for Black Enterprise Magazine's Financial Empowerment Series and The Hip-Hop Summit Action Network's Get Your Money Right series created by Russell Simmons and Dr. Benjamin Chavis.

Carmen is the Co-Founder of the first Black Female Private Equity Firm in Texas, Rhodium Capital Management. She has always been passionate about informing and educating her community. Carmen feels Rhodium is a conduit for creating and transferring intergenerational wealth in women and minority owned businesses.

Inspirational Message by
Gina Goree Hitchens

"Action without vision is only passing time,
vision without action is merely daydreaming, but
vision with action can change the world."

NELSON MANDELA

*I*t's often said that while raising children, whether married or single, the days move at a snail pace, yet the years travel faster than the speed of light. This spoke to me. When I was married with two children, my life was all about them. Then poof... out of nowhere, I was an empty nester; *NO*, really, my nest was ***"Totally empty."*** I looked around and wondered when and how did this happen?

Then, I stumbled upon a mirror and really became confused. I wondered, who is that *Woman in the mirror?* Umm.

1. How did she get here?
2. What does she want to do NEXT?
3. Why is this important to her?
4. Can she even afford herself?

From what I remembered, she was an ambitious woman with dreams and goals. Upon a closer look, I began to get *Fired Up*, especially when she began to talk!

She loudly roared, girl, you were gifted with a voice-it is time to *WAKE UP* and *Unleash Your Undeniable Impact!*

Then I really got *FIRED UP* because I realized, **She was me!!!** My PURPOSE was calling, and I was ready to answer!

"For I know the plans I have for you, declares the Lord, plans to prosper you and not harm you, plans to give you hope and a future." *Jeremiah 29:11*

Am I talking to myself? Or are you looking in the mirror thinking, Who is She? There must be more? What's NEXT?

You know there is *PURPOSE* buried inside of you that is screaming, ready to be UNLEASHED! Now is the time to *Make a Bold Move* and *Unleash Your Undeniable Impact!* But first, create a plan and a strategy.

Simply put, Get **SMART** first!

Strategic. Get laser-focused on your vision. What gifts are you ready to "Unleash"? Write the vision and make it plain.

> *"A goal casually set and lightly taken is freely abandoned at the first obstacle."*
> *Zig Ziglar.*

Motivated. Before leaping into action, *"Be Still"* long enough to get connected to *"What and Who Motivates and Inspires You"*- your *"What"* your *"Why."* After all, this is your North Star, the fuel that will keep you motivated and focused.

> *"Take time to deliberate, but when the time for action arrives, stop thinking and go in." Andrew Jackson*

Accountable and Action-Oriented. Always ask yourself these two simple questions, "What do I need to do now? Then, what do I need to do next?" Then do it.

> *"The best time to plant a tree was 20 years*
> *ago. The second, best time is now."*
> Chinese Proverb

Resourceful. What are you working with? Take inventory of your gifts and talents.

Tribal. Your Success Circle is critical to your success; your tribe should include people that *Inspire you toward Your Greater.*

In closing, trust the process, enjoy the journey, and stay connected with *"The Woman in the Mirror."*

> "Honor your calling. Everyone has one. Trust your heart,
> and success will come to you." *Oprah Winfrey*

Gina Goree Hitchens

Gina is the Creator of SMART Women Finish Strong- a Financial Empowerment Community that helps women define their highest vision of success and map out clear strategies enabling them to comfortably *"Approach their Next Season with Added Confidence"* and confidently LEAD Like a Woman!

With 30+ years in a male-dominated industry, Gina is a Financial Planner; President of GHG Financial Planning, and a John Maxwell Certified Speaker, Trainer, and Coach. With many years of *Life Lessons*, she enjoys helping women entering a new *Chapter of Life* and need to make quick, bold, and tough financial decisions. She knows her - She is her!

After her 30+ year marriage ended in divorce, Gina had to *Rebuild her personal wealth* and *Redefine her Purpose*. This inspired her passion for empowering women with the confidence to *Recognize* and *Afford the Woman in the Mirror.*

Get the inspiration you need to LEAD Like a Woman! www. SMARTWomenLead.com

Dr. Vanessa Jenkins

"If you do not unleash your undeniable impact, you will cripple your present and paralyze your future."

DR. VANESSA JENKINS

What is holding you back from taking the next step? What is your excuse this time? Let me guess. I am not good enough. I cannot do it. Who will follow me? I do not feel I am good enough. I do not have the money. I don't, and I can't are words we say all the time when we are at the point of taking our next step(s). Isn't it interesting we very rarely say I can, or I will? People and experiences can determine if you will take the risk or embrace a situation. This reminds me of the story of the elephant chained to the tent at the circus. The elephant does not realize the power he has. He has been conditioned to stay and not move, and based on previous experiences, when he did move, he suffered uncomfortable consequences. If he were to move his leg, the entire tent would fall, but because he has been conditioned not to move, he does not realize the power he has within. While there are many reasons why we are afraid to unleash our God-given purpose, there are four steps that can assist with unleashing your undeniable impact:

Step 1: Element all negative thoughts you have about whatever it is you are going to do and replace it with a positive.

Step 2: Address any fear(s) you may have about your next step. Keep in mind that FEAR is a distraction that prevents you from unleashing your full potential.

Step 3: Develop a plan for how you will address the next step, new project, or challenge, etc.

Step 4: Believe that you can do it. Remember, you have the power within to do whatever you want.

Knowing your "Y" plays a major role in unleashing your undeniable impact. Knowing your "Y" fuels your purpose and gives you power. It allows you to be grounded, especially if you are faced with decisions, challenges, next steps, uncertainties, etc. Think of life as a hill. We all know the challenges of climbing, the burning of our thighs, tired of just climbing, rolling down, not feeling like climbing. This all represents challenges in life. Put your "Y" at the top of the hill, and when you feel the challenges of climbing (life events), look up at your "Y" and keep climbing. If you roll down, get up and keep climbing. Knowing your "Y" makes your "what" clear and helps you to strategize your "how" so that you can continue to walk in your purpose. Now go and unleash your undeniable Impact.

Dr. Vanessa Jenkins

Dr. Vanessa Jenkins (aka) Dr. V The "Y" Strategist is the CEO/President of Dr. V Solutions, a subsidiary of Sentencing Options LLC in Norfolk, Virginia. Dr. V Solutions provides coaching, speaking, and training to individuals, organizations, businesses, and churches. Dr. V is known for her signature training on *What's Your "Y"* and *In Pursuit of Me*. For other services provided, please visit drvsolutions.org or follow me on Instagram @drvsolutions.

Inspirational Message by
Safiya Johnson

"Hands without battle scars are too weak to truly lay hold on the magnitude of the blessings ahead."

SAFIYA JOHNSON

Your struggle enables your victory! On any quest to greatness, you *will* encounter challenges, pain, and disappointment. It is not a likelihood of life, but a promise, because greatness favors the brave and the consistent. It is reserved for those who refuse to give in.

The purpose of this chapter is to reframe your share of life's difficulties. Each one is a divinely placed training program to give you the perfect combination of skills, knowledge, strength, and tenacity needed to fulfill your assignment in this generation. Every single pushback, setback, loss, heartbreak is meant to work *for* you, not against you.

Every so often, I think back to 2012 – the year that broke me. Or so I thought. That year, my two businesses crashed, my home was foreclosed, and I was diagnosed with a medical illness. I lost hundreds of thousands of dollars. Each new day was torture with mounting debt, no income, and a weak body. The tears, shame, and overwhelm were constant. But, deep within me, my God-given purpose, like a little flame, refused to die. I knew I was born for greatness – just as you are! So, my one intent is to fan your flame until it becomes a wildfire that you can no longer withstand. My hope is that you will be driven to break all barriers, shatter all glass ceilings, and unleash your undeniable impact!

There is one thing in common with those who have impacted the world: they have all lived through catastrophic difficulties. In fact, one wealth and marketing strategist, Dan Kennedy, said, "it was found that a significant number of legendary entrepreneurs have bankruptcies in their past." Your difficulty puts you in great company. You are well poised to make a legendary impact. Nothing you face or have faced – having no money, being a single parent, having no college degree, losing a loved one, or anything else – disqualifies you from setting the world ablaze. In fact, it is exactly that which qualifies you.

Your purpose is attached to your pain. If you are called to speak, life will tell you to keep quiet. If you are called to write, life will tell you don't even touch that pen. If you are called to impact the world, life will push you into a box. Life is not against you. Life is meant to qualify you, just like that butterfly that must struggle to break free of the cocoon to develop strong enough wings to take flight. Any butterfly that refuses to engage in that struggle will soon die or never see the beauty in the world that awaits it. No struggle, no victory. Albert Einstein said, "it's not that I'm so smart, it's just that I stay with problems longer."

In the end, every struggle won is a struggle your children and those behind you do not have to fight. So, fight with dignity and an assurance that your impact will change your world and theirs. Greatness awaits you!

Safiya Johnson

Safiya helps executives, especially millennials, exceed their career goals and still have a life. She knows what it takes to rise through the leadership ranks and impress her toughest critics as a young executive. Being inducted into the C-suite in her early 20s, Safiya had a stellar corporate career, including pioneering a massive portfolio of projects valued in excess of US$1.5 Billion, which included signature national projects that have reaped significant annual profits - all the while single handedly raising her son and enjoying thriving out-of-work activities. Safiya believes that no one should have to choose between being successful and their personal lives and developed a practical, winning leadership strategy to accomplish just that.

Safiya is also the founder of Safiya Group, a business support agency that provides specialist services in accounting, human resources, and strategic planning.

To find out more about Safiya and her work, visit www.SafiyaJohnson. com and www.SafiyaGroup.com.

Inspirational Message by
Glory-Anne Jones

"Nobody's gonna know...
about the unseen worries, the stomach-tightening apprehension,
the foundation-shaking doubt, and the breathtaking uncertainty.

Nobody's gonna know...
about how you poured your heart and soul into
your dreams to achieve your goals.

Nobody's gonna truly, deeply, and yes madly know...
except YOU—you will know."

GLORY-ANNE JONES

I'm sure you've heard this before, and maybe you've even thought about it yourself. Everyone wants someone to root for them. And to this, I say, get yourself in the company of someone like me -- the cheerleader. Back in the day, I was a cheerleader for our high school football and basketball teams. Because I was tiny, I was a "flyer," one who gets spectacularly thrown in the air reaching for even higher heights to be seen. (Get yourself a flyer!) As a cheerleader, my teammates and I worked on flashy stunts and created body-shaking dance routines. This was and is a serious sport.

Why do you need a cheerleader? As I see it, the cheerleader has three jobs. One is to react to the work players are doing on the field and court. On the 30-yard line? "Move that ball, team; we want a 1st down!" On the 10-yard line? "Go for goal team; we want more!" Making your way down the court? "Swishhhhh, two points a basket, sink that ball!" We weren't out there telling them how to run patterns. We weren't out there calling the shots. We were highlighting the moves the teams made.

How does that relate to you today? Get yourself a cheerleader who is right there next to you. They will celebrate the work before, during and after you achieve your first, second, third (and more) goals. The trip from premiering on the entrepreneurial field to finally crushing your first goal (and others) is a journey full of nerves, worries, and apprehension. From the sidelines, your cheerleader will witness your work, and regardless of gains or losses, will be there to encourage you.

The second job a cheerleader has is to keep the crowd engaged and hyped. We are your brand ambassadors. Before being an influencer was a thing, we did the pregame show, the halftime show, and went wild with you and the crowd when the game was over.

Today your cheerleader goes into the group of potential customers and clients to spread the excitement. They can create positive momentum with insight into how absolutely fantastic it can be to work with you. Piquing interest and creating FOMO (fear of missing out), your cheerleader engages, entertains, and excites.

Lastly, as varsity cheerleaders, we shined on our own, representing our school. (This is important as it's a trait you will want to make sure your cheerleader has.) We had our training camps, daily practices, and competitions. We had our own identity. During games, we were the bridge between the players and the crowd. We were the connecting force that held space between the bleachers and field or court.

Your cheerleader has work to do and will not be "all up in your business." The singular most important reason to have one of your own is to help bring you closer to your potential clients and customers in a positive way.

Don't delay; get yourself a cheerleader. Then, get your game on!

Glory-Anne Jones

Hi, I'm Glory-Anne Jones, emotional life coach (6 years) and founder of Chocolate is Self-Care, the chocolate tea company (launched 3/8/21). Emotions truly dictate our success or failure. It's imperative that we thoughtfully consider them in our business plans. If you feel overwhelmed by self-doubt and fall into a cycle of self-sabotage, it seems impossible to break through. Everyone can reach deep down and unleash caged confidence and courage. Positive emotions can catapult you higher and higher. I can be your cheerleader every step of the way. The tea company was born out of personal frustration. Clients would say, "I'm sorry, I didn't have time to take care of myself this week." My reply is, "you can't pour from an empty pitcher." I created signature chocolate tea blends as a recharge mode, so people can fill up their cups. In the process, they can find the quiet time to contemplate and connect. hello@gloryannejones.com, www.gloryannejones.com, www.chocolateisselfcare.com

Inspirational Message by
Moirar M. Leveille

"Let your pain increase your vision, become your source of inspiration and empowerment to transform and uplift the spirit of the wounded."

MOIRAR M. LEVEILLE

No man is an island; true, but I'd rather you focus on my sovereignty and not my solitariness. It is a no-brainer; we innately want to find a sense of belonging amongst these earthly mercurial beings, find footing lest we slip through the cracks. It's appalling that we morph into butterflies for other people's pleasure, never knowing beauty from our own eyes. This glass jar we're in is as safe as it is toxic; we better break the glass and burn up before we burn out. Our potential is an illuminating light their eyes could never carry, so why hold it under the water, fearing that they'll go blind? The masses love to feast on fear, so best believe they will dine on your potential if you don't show up dressed in a smirk. Let your mighty little voice lead the way, carving out the undeniable you just like I did.

A while ago, my body started to whisper ever so slightly that I brushed it off as quickly as I did my mundane thoughts. The whisper soon turned into sirens, but even the doctors dubbed its bright colors as normal and my concerns as constant complaints. My body chowed itself, over time attacking its own cells and tissues until it was excruciatingly painful to remain silent. I was finally diagnosed with an autoimmune disease.

My body was literally telling me to speak up and speak out for myself lest this very gift of life withers from inside out. My body became vocal when it came to its needs, and my mind could either follow suit or arbitrarily remain num like it was used to.

As I began my medication, I also began the change of mind, stripping the silence I had borrowed from the world in the form of fear of other people's perception of me. Inertia became my second nature, and it was time to ignite this stubborn gas. I stopped listening to my diagnosis so I could hear the whispers of my intuition first. Patience and grit were a choice I made every waking day, yielding a new identity that could only be defined by me. It took my brokenness for me to realize what being whole felt like. I charged beyond self-neglect to achieve the realization and actualization of self-care. My inner shambles built a functional medicine practitioner.

The secret of being empowered lies in the doing. The only way to acquire that identity is to start living it. Running a mile daily clears the clutter upstairs as it does the weight, making space for stronger thoughts and drive. Eating healthy builds a sound ability to choose wellness over instant gratification that chips you away for years. The little thoughts we ignore become the building blocks of who we are while shaping the world's view of us. Your impact can only go as far as your thoughts. Until then, the power within will be unleashed because success starts with self-care, and it's your responsibility.

Moirar M. Leveille

Moirar is a Mindset and Wellness Therapist. She is LMHC, a three-time international bestselling author, a clinical Iridologist, and a functional medicine practitioner, Life and Wellness Coach. She is the founder and CEO of Moirar Holistic Wellness, and she is currently Pursuing her Ph.D. and doctorate in Integrative Medicine.

She uses five languages to create everlasting personal transformation by helping people access their intrinsic personal power to overcome emotional barriers, fight chronic diseases, reduce stress and enhance the quality of life and achieve their highest potential to live with vibrancy and passion.

She shares her passion for life after facing her death prescription. She lives to Inspire, Empower and Transform lives. She reminds us that we always have access to the Reset Button and where there's a will, there is a way.

Find her at www.moirar.com or at tlc@moirar.com.

Inspirational Message by
Charlene Love

"We're not defined by our circumstances, and we can always find a way to rise above it."

ASHLEIGH MURRAY

*A*re you ready to pep up, step up, and rise up in your career? Do you want a makeover to advance over into a career you have been desiring for a while? If you are agitated, rejected, and stuck, and do not know how to overcome workplace barriers, achieve career growth and positive transformation, you do not have to remain stagnant because of your circumstances.

Let me tell you about something authentic, genuine, good, and sensational. Well, it is called an unstoppable career affair. Yes, you heard right. This unstoppable career affair is mentally, spiritually, and emotionally attractive to a person's career satisfaction; and, guess what? It's true to you.

The good news is, if desirable, you can have an unstoppable career affair, too, and let me clarify what I am referring to upfront. Live, love, like, and listen, plus learn about the things you do professionally and embrace the unstoppable career affair (pertaining to career work performances, taking actions, and being dutiful) to persevere beyond heightened levels of success.

The affair involves a person who is in pursuit of being unstoppable in achieving success in his or her career by measuring up and moving forward into greatness. In your career, you want to be committed and dedicated to the purpose of why you are there. While every day is not peachy creamy, each day is a fresh start to a new beginning in your professional life.

Would you like to be relentless, unshakeable, invincible, and determined in your career? I will elaborate on the key components to encourage you to proactively 'win' in your career. The three imperative ways are: 1) Pep Up, 2) Step Up, and 3) Rise Up.

Pep Up and feel inspired, ignited, and invigorated in your career. Having a renewed mindset and being motivated will cause you to expend good feelings and display a positive attitude. Step Up and climb the ladder of success by taking strides to move upward with purposeful objectives. Rise Up and reach above the horizon as you navigate your value, education, job experiences, accomplishments, certifications, and achievements to accelerate your career win.

I believe when people live the life they desire and love the way it makes them feel, they will begin to like their careers and reach forward with the probability of advancement into a favorable, fulfilling, and rewarding future. Also, it is beneficial to listen to sound and quality discussions, which may launch an intentional makeover to move over into a new position. Give yourself private space to learn everything about the career position or job and precisely see the big picture you have been focusing on.

You have the capabilities and tenacity to overcome your fears and setbacks and rise above your circumstances to reach career goals or dreams. So, please do goodwill for yourself and get in gear to Pep Up, Step Up, and Rise Up to a victorious career. You deserve the best. You are a champion winner!

Charlene Love

Charlene Love is a highly experienced Career Coach and CEO of Love Career Business and also a licensed minister. Charlene established her company to assist employees and executives in moving forward in their careers, preparing for mid-level and senior-level advancement, and demolishing barriers that have kept them stuck and stagnant in their current positions. Charlene is aware of the challenges and setbacks that people encounter in their careers. She understands your pain, struggles, and frustrations because she had to persevere through some similar situations working in corporate America for numerous organizations.

As a career coach, Charlene is passionate about helping clients who are agitated, rejected and stuck, make the change to overcome workplace barriers, achieve career growth, and positive transformation. Charlene enjoys teaching professionals how to transition from one career to another career, and helping them excel into greatness. Charlene offers group coaching or individual sessions.

Please visit www.lovecareerbusiness.com

Inspirational Message by
Sabrina Lowery

"Your Vibe Attracts Your Tribe."

UNKNOWN

There are people in the world who leave a lasting impression on you while impressing you with their creativity and vibrant energy. Well, I am one of those people. I'm a Jersey girl whose energy is electrifying and contagious. I remember being a very happy little girl full of energy, running around making my family and friends laugh and smile all the time. I loved exploring new technologies, and I have had all the new gadgets since the 1970s, when computers were born. I dreamed about working at NASA. I wanted to be one of the 1st black women to launch a space shuttle. I used to spend hours at the arcade playing games with my friends. But then I answered my calling without even knowing it. I stopped hanging out with my friends playing games at the arcade, and spending money, and I decided that I wanted to learn how to code the games and make all that money. We used to spend $5.00 or $10.00 every time we went to the arcade. I remember rolling quarters before school some mornings to meet up with my cousins and friends at the arcade. I asked Mommy to enroll me in a BASIC coding class, and she said "yes."

That's when I began to walk in my purpose. Mommy ALWAYS made me read. I can remember when I started reading books about coding and putting in hours of work in the computer lab while my friends were hanging out and parlaying. I used to be envious of them having fun all the time. I had become a serial entrepreneur by the time I was in high school. I would learn just about anything and perfect it. I baked cookies, I learned how to cut and braid hair, I learned how to do acrylic nails, I learned how to dance and sing, I learned how to code, I learned three languages, I learned to speak professionally on stages, and the list goes on. I learned very early that I could make money doing something that is easy for me by helping someone who might not find that thing easy. That's when I learned that by using my creativity and innovation, my vibrant personality, AND my voice, that I could unleash my undeniable gifts and talents to make an extraordinary impact in the world.

Say "yes" to those things that are uncomfortable and different. Sacrifice those things which are non-income generating activities to develop those skills that will help build your legacy. You have to say "yes" to those opportunities when no one else will. You must ask for the help you need. I've learned to surround myself with like-minded people, creative thinkers, thought leaders, and people who are using their voices to *be the change they wish to see in the world*," which is my favorite quote by Mahatma Gandhi. You should do the same. Unleash your undeniable impact on the world. Your audience is waiting.

Sabrina Lowery

Sabrina Lowery is a serial MOMpreneur with three sons and over 20 revenue streams. Sabrina is the Chief Technology Officer for Sabrina Lowery Enterprises, LLC, known as the "Tech Evangelist." As a Certified Google Digital Coach and Certified Microsoft Innovative Educator since 2015, Sabrina launched The Geek Tank Academy in 2018. Lowery is also the best-selling author of "*The Entrepreneur's Blueprint for Digital Dominance*" and "*Social eTECHquette: Communicating with a Conscious Mindset.*"

Mrs. Lowery is the Qualifying Broker of Legacy Realty & Management, LLC based in Atlanta, GA, recognized as the 2015 Businesswoman of the Year for Outstanding Achievement by Atlanta Business League for generating over 7-figures in her first years of business. Lowery is certified by Cornell University in Women's Entrepreneurship and is an award-winning Leader, Influencer, Innovative Technologist, and mogul in the real estate industry since 2003. Learn more about Sabrina at www.sabrinalowery.com

Miriam Matthews, LICSW

"Your PAST is your PUSH, for your PURPOSE!"

MIRIAM MATTHEWS, LICSW

Would have, should have, could have, I give up, I don't care anymore, I'm not special…….STOP. I know you've experienced challenges. Many of the challenges, negative experiences, or TRAUMAS that you endured sent painful messages. We consciously and unconsciously process those challenges in a way, in which we feel defines our existence. Perhaps you formed negative or limiting beliefs about who you are. You may have even been told what you are not, or maybe you've been compared by someone you love, so therefore you compare yourself now. This leaves you with a constant feeling of deficiency.

You may feel that any rejection or disappointment you've experienced is indicative of your value. Well, I'm here to tell you to pause and think of your favorite fictional story or movie. Why? The story you have been telling yourself about your low self-worth and lack of value is NO different from a story based on fiction! The fictional story is simply not TRUE. It's not the events or mistakes that keep us trapped! It's the lies that we tell ourselves about who we are that keep us trapped in stagnation. I came to liberate you today with the truth, and the truth shall set you free! If you've ever experienced a challenge, you have value! If you've ever experienced pain, you have value! If you've ever experienced shame, you have value! If you've ever experienced rejection, you have value! If you've ever made a mistake, you have value! Why? Because with those experiences come lessons and knowledge!

Choosing to identify with the lesson and not the pain changes your trajectory towards the path of empowerment! If you even have ONE lesson you've learned, you have value, and someone else can benefit from your lesson. You are not the negative event that happened to you; you are the resilience that rose above it! Stop delaying your greatness. Kobe Bryant said, *"The mistake that many people make is thinking we have time!"* Well, NOW is the time for you to listen to this message of possibility and begin speaking possibility into your own life! Matthew 19:26 says, *"With God, all things are possible!"* I challenge you to step in faith and deepen your spiritual walk.

Access instantaneous grace, infinite love, and possibility. You've ALWAYS been fearfully and wonderfully made. Your thirst to be great is inherently designed and a part of your DNA. It can only be quenched by stepping into your purpose! You've learned lessons that have strengthened your resilience, and there are mountains that only YOU are uniquely qualified to climb! Choose to do it, and you will be successful! Falling as you climb is okay, as long as you keep going. There's a mountain with ONLY your name on it. At the top of each mountain are individuals waiting ON YOU, FOR YOUR HELP and GUIDANCE. Climb, AND Unleash your UNDENIABLE impact!

Miriam Matthews, LICSW

My name is Miriam Matthews, and I am a Licensed Independent Clinical Social Worker. I began my Social Work career in 2008. However, I began to fulfill my purpose in advocacy and helping others at a young age. I always knew that I wanted to help others, and the stars aligned as I discovered behavioral and mental health. I am passionate about facilitating each individual's breakthroughs! It's an honor to be an integral part of each person's cultivation of their belief in themselves and Divine faith. I've greatly enjoyed working with women to help them redefine who they are by their standards and develop a positive new relationship with themselves. I am excited about God's Divine assignment on my life in helping others heal. For help with processing your past, to push towards your purpose, visit my website, resourcefulblossoming. com.

Follow me on social media: https://www.instagram.com/defineyourdna/.

Inspirational Message by
Wendy Garvin Mayo, APRN, ANP-BC

"Be Your BEST, Do Your BEST, Give Your BEST"

WENDY GARVIN-MAYO

You were uniquely created and chosen to occupy the space where you stand today. You possess the POWER to illuminate the lives of people who have the privilege to experience you. You have an added value - that intangible "thing" you do that internally lights you up and touches people in ways they did not even know they needed to be touched - that can transform the world, one person at a time.

In March 2020, my added value was challenged as I sat on the couch breastfeeding my newborn son while experiencing fear, stress, and indecision about returning to the hospital as an Oncology Nurse Practitioner during the COVID-19 pandemic. I pondered, do I honor my passion to serve as a nurse or allow the chaos to keep me mentally paralyzed. This indecision was suffocating my added value to radically serve and transform the lives of cancer patients. The decision was tough until I recalled the resounding words of a wise man, my grand-father, who once told me, " ...in this chapter of your life, you need to set your sail." Those words calmed the chaos and gave me clarity about returning to the hospital to stand with the many cancer patients who do not have a choice.

We often allow personal stressors to prohibit us from being our BEST, doing our BEST, and giving our BEST. Managing those stressors empowers us to tap into our added value, unleashing our undeniable impact. Normally, no one teaches us how to manage stress despite its negative impacts on all aspects of our lives. Especially our added value! The SHAPE framework helps us gain perspective and outline a plan to manage stressors:

1. Explore the **S**tory to understand the who, what, why, when, and how of your stressors to determine their impact on your life.
2. Imagine life if you **H**one in on accessing your added value.
3. **A**ssess what tools you have and what tools you require to manage your stressors.
4. Formulate a specific, measurable, attainable, realistic, and timed (SMART) **P**lan that utilizes the tools you identified to access your added value.
5. **E**xecute the plan today by committing to one thing you can do for five days to operationalize your plan.

What stressors are holding you back from using the POWER of your added value to unleash your undeniable impact? Use the SHAPE framework as a guide to managing your stressors and uncovering your added value because we, the world, are waiting for **YOU**!

Wendy Garvin Mayo, APRN, ANP-BC

Board-Certified Nurse Practitioner || Stress Solution Strategist || Author || International Speaker || Certified John Maxwell Coach & Trainer

Wendy Garvin Mayo is the Founding CEO of The Stress Blueprint, creator of the Nurse Wellness Mentorship, host of the Nurse Wellness Podcast, and inventor of the SHAPE framework. Her mission is to empower nurses to manage stress to amplify their personal and professional development. She has over 20 years of experience in healthcare in various nursing sectors such as clinical, leadership, research, academia, and pharmaceuticals.

Wendy serves as a member of The American Institute of Stress Daily Life & Workplace Stress board, advisor for the Johnson & Johnson nursing employee resource group, sits on the Board of Directors for the Connecticut League for Nursing and President of Central Connecticut Oncology Nursing Society.

Wendy is available for speaking, training, and coaching opportunities. For more information, visit www.stressblueprint.com or email hello@stressblueprint.com

Inspirational Message by
Latrece Williams McKnight

"Don't be pushed around by the fears in your
mind. Be led by the dreams in your heart."

ROY T. BENNETT

Dreams have enormous power. Think about the dreams that reside deep within your heart. They mean a great deal to you, or you wouldn't hang on to them, right? Well, it may only be a very short time before they come to pass. And even if their fulfillment is a long way away, hold on to those dreams as you experience progress towards them.

When the time is right - and when you're ready - your dreams will be realized. In the meantime, you can *unleash* the power that your dreams offer you. But how do you do that?

Do your dreams bring you wealth? Health? Love? Something else? Whatever means the most to you and brings you immeasurable joy will often appear in your dreams.

Your dreams might not even be for you. They might be for someone else. You can bring joy, love and light to many people by using the power of your dreams for the good of others. You can teach others to realize their dreams and *unleash* that power as well.

Dream a Powerful Dream

Your big picture goals can keep you going. They provide motivation and fuel for life. Many settle for less than the best life they can live, but you can decide today that you'll accept no less than the fulfillment of your dreams.

The key, keep putting one foot in front of the other, taking small steps in the direction of your dreams. At the same time, continually visualize what your life looks like at the finish line. *As you complete each step along the way, you'll gain more power to complete the rest of your journey.*

You may have a setback or two before you see your dream completely realized. That's normal. Roadblocks only serve to show you the strength of your desire for this dream's fulfillment.

You can *unleash* the power of your dreams by:

- Taking small steps each day toward their fulfillment
- Using them for your own joy and the joy and good of others
- Turning a small dream into a large one by thinking big
- Staying brave and courageous when challenges come
- Spending time with people who are encouraging and helpful
- Encouraging others to follow their dreams and realize their desires

Always Remember the Power of the Dream

Your dreams are an extension and expression of who you are. When you dream something, give it everything you've got and see it through until your dream is fulfilled. *The only thing stopping you from achieving your most important dreams is you!* Refuse to accept defeat and resolve to keep taking action to get what you want until you achieve the victory you deserve.

Dreams have power, but you must continue to feed them. Do everything you can to realize your dream by taking massive, consistent action. As you go, notice what is working and what isn't. Adjust your course continually, and nothing can stop you from experiencing the realization of the dreams that you hold in your heart.

Latrece Williams McKnight

Minister Latrece Williams McKnight is the Founder President/CEO of Mcknight Williams & Associates, LLC, President of Real Success University, Creator of Gospelology and Author of seven best seller books. Her passion is your success. Latrece is a dynamic children's and youth ministry speaker, consultant, and leader. To many churches and organizations around the world, she is known as the "Children's Ministry Guru". She inspires and provides tools for youth leaders and volunteers to achieve great success in their lives and reach children for change.

She has been recognized throughout organizations for her ability to motivate, connect with and energize her audience into action. Latrece has traveled to five continents, Africa, Asia, Europe, North America, and South America, teaching youth leaders the gospel of Jesus Christ. Her most recent trips to Uganda allowed Latrece the honor to teach over 5,000 youth and to train over 200 pastors and youth ministry workers.

IG: @MsLatrece

Inspirational Message by
Rachelle Middleton

"...And he that was dead came forth, bound hand and foot with graveclothes: and his face was bound about with a napkin. Jesus saith unto them, Loose him, and let him go."

JOHN 11:44 KJV

Let's take a moment to reacquaint ourselves with the word **Unleash**. A word that we hear often but *may* not always pull it in close to allow it to truly resonate.

Two simple parts that carry the power of turning an idea 180 degrees. The prefix **Un** means to do the opposite and create a reversal, which means even though you are scared to ask for that promotion or scared to leave that relationship, you do it anyway.

The suffix **leash** literally means a state of being restrained or bound for the purpose of controlling. What are you allowing to hold you back from your purpose? It's time to put these two powerful words together and unleash.

Unleash what you have not for yourself but for those who are assigned to you. For example, my unleashing led me to you. At this moment, as I'm typing these words, I don't see myself as a writer. Yet, you are reading the words of a best seller!

By no means do I have it all together. As a matter of fact, from the surface, it looks just the opposite. I experienced a "failed marriage." I'm a single mother of (2) "grown" teenagers. The dating scene isn't at all what I expected and on top of that, I was released from my management position right before the biggest pandemic of our lifetime. I tell you this not for pity but to let you know that in spite of it all, I found the capacity to create who I want to be and you can too. The only person that you need to convince... is you!

Once I truly embraced the power I held to unleash the non-serving things and pursue the life I wanted, it was only a few months before I began to see everything I've ever wanted begin to manifest.

It started with me actively retraining my thoughts. I know this doesn't apply to you because those reading this book have it all together... right? As my Pastor would say, "just keep looking ahead!" For me, the whispers in my head were louder than any words of my frenemies. My words were contradicting what I desired

"Im not qualified"
"I'm too old"
"I don't deserve it"

These were all scripts I recited unconsciously that pulled me away from what I was pursuing. After all, if I didn't believe in myself, why would someone else?

The frustration of this and quite frankly, the exhaustion pushed me to rewrite my S.T.O.R.Y. and change how I spoke over my life, my health and my future.

Let me be your witness that YOU CAN do it too!

Remember, to unleash is to allow or cause something very powerful to happen suddenly. When that negative thinking comes up, affirm yourself with positivity. When your health is a concern, yes, go to the doctor but speak healing over your body. When a big opportunity comes your way, it's ok to be scared, but do it anyway!

Rachelle Middleton

Rachelle is an entrepreneur, published best-selling author, motivational speaker, and established accountability coach. She is also the CEO and founder of InCourage, a world-class organization that inspires safe, cycle-breaking, courageous conversations that help others get an overall improved quality of both their mental and physical state.

Rachelle is not only a dynamic leader in her community, but she is also the mother of two inspiring young women who are also paving the way as the next generation of influential world-shakers.

Born and raised in Los Angeles, California, Rachelle is an advocate for mental health and in constant pursuit of building community through the vehicles of psychology and understanding trauma.

Rachelle believes that her purpose is the solution and makes it her mission to encourage those around her to embrace who they are by providing the tools necessary to find the courage from within.

For more information, visit our website at incouragewithin.com or follow Rachelle @incourage_within.

Inspirational Message by
Jen Mighty

"Sometimes when things seem to be falling to pieces, they are really falling into place."

UNKNOWN

July 14, 2009, I was driving on a quiet street in Connecticut when I spotted a car exiting a driveway and knew the driver saw me, as I am *certain* she looked at me. Suddenly she was driving into my path, and with nowhere to go, I swerved left, then right to avoid hitting a metal pole head-on! My car flipped, and I was upside down! I know it was less than 10 minutes, but in that position, it felt like forever! It seemed surreal! During it all, there was a weird calm within me. I knew *God got me*! Surprisingly, I escaped with only three torn rotator cuffs, for which I had surgery to repair.

Now, why do I share that story? For you to realize that even when life feels like it is upside down, things can still fall into place. Regardless of what is flipped in your life right now, you can get through it. In fact, I was also in the middle of a divorce with a 6-year-old child in the mix. Yep! Talk about life flipping upside down!!

That accident confirmed for me that there was something here for me to do! It is true, "Sometimes when things seem to be falling to pieces, they are really falling into place." I recognized that the ONLY reason I was still here, the ONLY reason I came out almost unscathed, was because my assignment was incomplete! This life, MY life, had purpose!!

"If you are breathing, your assignment is incomplete!" You have purpose!!

Now I don't know what that is for you, but know, your situation does not determine your elevation!! Use your challenges as stepping stones into your greatness and the impact you are here to create!

You may be one of two people reading this right now. 1. You know what you want but are not sure how to move forward or are too afraid to pursue it, and 2. You have no idea what "It" is. Either way, it's time to ACT!

A: Acknowledge the fear but decide you will not live there! It is ok to be afraid, but face the fear and do it anyway because that is the only way you will get the fulfillment you are seeking in this life!

C: Commit to being true to who and what you are by sharing your gifts with the world. Someone is waiting on your courage! Someone is stuck right now because YOU are the only one that can release them, with your message, with your gift.

T: Transform – It's in the transformation that everything happens. Align yourself with the coaches and support needed to guide you along your journey to purpose. Learn to be the best version of yourself, step outside your comfort zone and engage in all the ACTions necessary to walk into your divine purpose and create impact!!!

My question to you is, when will you begin to A.C.T. on your calling and unleash your undeniable Impact? Why not now?

Jen Mighty

Jennifer has a background in accounting and is the Finance Controller for a major Nonprofit organization after spending many years within a Fortune 100 company. Jennifer holds a bachelor's degree in Accounting and a Master of Science in Professional Accounting. She, however, has a passion for serving and has served in various capacities on several non-profit boards within the community. Jennifer is an entrepreneur and trains and mentors a team as an Independent Associate and Executive Director with LegalShield.

To further fulfill her passion for helping others, she created S.T.A.R. - Sisters Transforming And Rising. She also hosted the annual Connecticut Celebration of Women Brunch and Awards to target a larger audience from 2015 thru 2019. Her greatest accomplishment, however, is being a mother to her teenage son. It is her desire to continue to make an impact within her community and internationally. You may connect with her on IG @sisterstransformingandrising

Inspirational Message by
Evangelist Sherrell D. Mims

"No one can compete with me because I am the original DNA. Anyone else is just a duplicate model."

SHERRELL D. MIMS

These are words that I live by. As an essential frontline worker, I had to go into my workplace even when I didn't want to in order to take care of your loved ones so you didn't have to.

Every day I had to remind myself of God's promises in my heart; *"For all the promises of God in him are yea, and in him Amen, unto the glory of God by us."* I Corinthians 1:20 KJV

Do you know who you are? The two most powerful words in the English language are "I AM." Because what comes after I AM will shape your life. What you say after "I AM" … What you BELIEVE after "I AM" will control your decisions and shape your life
www.fearlessmotivation.com

You must choose your words wisely. Your words are powerful and lively. You want to always keep a positive outlook on what you say.

I challenge you for the next 30 days and beyond that, as you wake up every morning and look into the mirror, AFFIRM who you are? This will set the tone for your day, week, month, and year. Once I do my affirmations, I feel exuberated, powerful, euphoric. I am on a spiritual high, and I love it. I go into work illuminating, fierce, and ready. My coworkers would say, "here she comes, Mrs. Positive!"

Israel Houghton has a song out called; "I Know Who I Am." Take time to listen to it.

When you speak, speak life over every area of your life. Make sure that your heart is pure before you begin your affirmations; ask God, "create in me a clean heart, O God; and renew a right spirit within me." Psalms 51:10 KJV

Do this practical exercise with me. Close your eyes or look in a mirror and say out loud who you are. Remember, your words are life, and what you speak into the atmosphere will grow.

When you speak out these affirmations, I want you to speak with authority and boldness. Let's go! Here are just a few affirmations that I have created.

> I AM WHO GOD SAYS I AM.
> I AM FAVORED BY GOD.
> I AM BEAUTIFULLY AND WONDERFULLY MADE. (Psalms 139:4 KJV)
> I AM AN UNLEASHED, UNDENIABLE IMPACT.
> I AM LOVE.
> I AM RELENTLESS.
> I AM SUCCESSFUL.
> I AM VICTORIOUS.
> I AM A CHILD OF THE KING.
> I AM CHOSEN (John 15:16 KJV)
> I AM A SURVIVOR.
> I AM STILL STANDING.

I AM A POWER VOICE.

I AM PROUD OF WHO I AM.

Once you have spoken these affirmations, by all means, add in your own as well. You are what you speak out of your mouth.

Know who you are. Speak who you are, and be who you are.

"I AM DETERMINED TO DO MY VERY BEST"

~~Lailah Gifty Akita

Evangelist Sherrell D. Mims

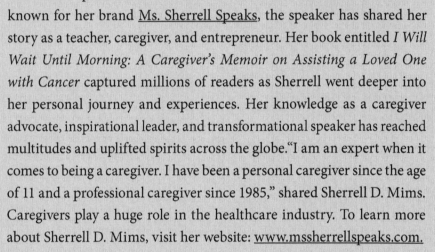

Evangelist Sherrell D. Mims is a bestselling author and contributor of several books that have captivated readers worldwide. Also known for her brand <u>Ms. Sherrell Speaks</u>, the speaker has shared her story as a teacher, caregiver, and entrepreneur. Her book entitled *I Will Wait Until Morning: A Caregiver's Memoir on Assisting a Loved One with Cancer* captured millions of readers as Sherrell went deeper into her personal journey and experiences. Her knowledge as a caregiver advocate, inspirational leader, and transformational speaker has reached multitudes and uplifted spirits across the globe. "I am an expert when it comes to being a caregiver. I have been a personal caregiver since the age of 11 and a professional caregiver since 1985," shared Sherrell D. Mims. Caregivers play a huge role in the healthcare industry. To learn more about Sherrell D. Mims, visit her website: <u>www.mssherrellspeaks.com.</u>

Email:<u>mssherrellspeaks@aol.com</u>
Follow on social media:
<u>https://www.facebook.com/</u>Sherrell.Baker
https://instagram.com/mssherrellspeak

Inspirational Message by
Cheryl Minnette

"Trauma can put you on a crash course to your destiny."

CHERYL MINNETTE

Who goes to work and shortly after arriving your sight disappears? No warning, seeing blood and boom...it's gone!! We all have a story that has changed our outlook and trajectory in life in one way or another. Whatever your story or mess was, it's not so much about it, as it is about YOU, so unleash it.

When you're up to bat and life throws you a fast ball that hits you dead-on, dropping you like a sack of potatoes, what's next? It's not the trauma that defines you. You are defined by your next action or lack of action. The choice you make can be critical.

Whenever you have a devastating life moment, it may affect you mentally, physically, financially, etc. This is when you need to A.C.T. Now is the time because there has been a shift in your world. What was is no longer. Prior to starting back up, you need to view your situation from a new vantage point. Honing your mental strength for focus, clarity, and faith to draw out your inner power as you strengthen your resilience is key.

Are you willing to walk on the path of 'no more excuses'
or stay on the side of doubt and hopelessness?

If you are propelled into a new life chapter, then slam into a fork in the road, which way would you go? Would you go left and sit in the mess of woe you see growing rampant? OR, would you go right into uncharted, unknown territory where growth may begin? This is when A.C.T. comes into play, so let's break it down a bit.

A - Assess:

Here is where you reflect on the trauma that occurred. You will need to gain an understanding as to why this occurrence happened. In addition, know where you are now, in this present moment. Your assessment includes all things, including the people around you.

C - Create a Plan:

Take your previous assessment, with all its layers and extensions, and lay them before you. Map out a strategy that will propel you in the direction of your true passion. Having a blueprint outlines your path.

T - Take Action:

Here is where you get into motion, by actively executing the steps laid out in your plan. This is the hardest part of the A.C.T. 1) Having the fortitude to act in the aftermath, 2) boldly stepping into unknown territory, 3) Staying focused on seeing beyond your current circumstances, while knowing you are still in the present. Truly a test of your mental strength and inner power.

Your time is now; honor it! Many people don't survive. Having tools in your personal toolbox is a must. Using them requires execution. You can jumpstart your life onto the path you are destined to walk upon. Staying the course with all the rigorous challenges that life throws at you takes skill. With your mental strength and inner power, you can achieve and succeed with great impact.

Cheryl Minnette

Cheryl Minnette, a courageous mother and businesswoman whose world was forever changed. One morning she left for work, returning home without her eyesight. Her world imploded and devastated the people around her. Now dealing with blindness and more, Cheryl was determined to 'walk the walk' to visually demonstrate for her children 'the talk' she was always teaching them. "Trust in your abilities, even when life serves you scraps." She was determined not to allow herself to be written off. Instead, she began writing her own chapter.

With decades of business and extraordinary life experiences, Cheryl began delving into the online world. She has become a Motivational speaker, Best-selling author, and the creator and host of The Cooking Blind Kitchen. She is the CEO of Vision Navigation Consulting, named Woman On The Move, and honored by Women Thriving Fearlessly. Learn more, contact Cheryl at eyelivelifetoo@gmail.com

Dr. Theresa A. Moseley

"Recognize that every interaction you have is an
opportunity to make a positive impact on others."

SHEP HYKEN

I recognized the power that we have when we interact with our family, friends, and community. We have the power to impact their lives positively. Every interaction has a purpose. There is a reason why we are communicating, networking, and dialoguing. It's important that we make this opportunity a positive one. Words are very powerful. No matter the situation you are addressing, your words can resolve the problem and have a positive outcome. However, the key to making the interaction positive is the words that you use. Your tone and overall presentation are important too. If you want to Unleash Your Undeniable Impact, you must speak up and speak out. You never know who you may help work through a problem by listening to what you have to say.

I remember August of 1965 in Fayetteville, North Carolina. My mother went to Haymount Elementary School to register her five children. Prior to this, we walked three miles to and from school every day. Haymount was close to our neighborhood and the home school for our address. When she went to register us, she was denied because of the color of our skin. My mother immediately went to the superintendent and unleashed her undeniable impact. She told the superintendent that her husband fought in two wars, he was a United States Army Soldier, he pays property tax at 1107 Chesterfield Drive, which is in Haymount's district. She told him that if he did not register her kids, she would call the President of the United States because separate is not equal. With his nice southern drawl, the superintendent immediately called the secretary at Haymount Elementary and told her to register the Moseley's immediately.

The rest is history. We went to integrated schools in elementary, middle, and high schools. My mother unleashed her undeniable impact. I continue her legacy as I realized that my voice is my gift. Using my voice, I am changing the world around me. I speak on love, peace, passion, and purpose. Everybody has a gift that will impact the world. It's meant for you to share through your passion and purpose. Jane Goodall, a scientist, conservationist, and peacemaker, said, "You cannot get through a single day without having an impact on the world around you. What you do makes a difference, and you have to decide what kind of difference you want to make." What will you do today and the rest of your life to unleash your undeniable impact? I encourage you to look inside your heart and mind and deliver your undeniable impact. We are all here for a reason. We were designed to serve the world. Remember, the interactions you have with others are an opportunity to have an undeniable impact.

Dr. Theresa A. Moseley

Dr. Theresa A. Moseley is originally from Fayetteville, North Carolina. She is a United States Army Veteran, motivational speaker, International Best Selling Author, and 3x Best-Selling Author. Dr. Moseley is the owner and CEO of TAM Creating Ambassadors of Peace LLC. She speaks and writes on passion, purpose, and peace. She uses her life experiences to address thought-provoking questions around finding one's purpose in life, finding your authentic self, and is very overt regarding everyone taking responsibility for creating a peaceful world.

Dr. Moseley has worked in the field of education for 26 years. She is a 3x Award-Winning Educator, including Maryland EGATE Gifted and Talented Administrator 2012. Dr. Moseley attended summer programs at Harvard Graduate School of Education. Leadership: An Evolving Vision and Institute on Critical Issues in Urban Special Education.

Dr. Moseley's events and access to her social media sites are available on her website, creatingambassadorsofpeace.com.

Inspirational Message by
Jori Mundy

"You were made for your journey."

JORI MUNDY

This world hasn't even experienced the ripple effect of what you have inside of you. You've been tested, doubted yourself, wondered if everything would work out, and yet here you are reading this book because deep down inside of you, you know you must keep moving. You haven't given up regardless of the challenges and uncertainties that lied ahead.

I remember the night my mother laid on her deathbed. She was in the intensive care unit fighting for her life after having a massive stroke. All the years preceding that day, she expressed the importance of finishing what you start, giving your all to what you do, and becoming the best at it. She established the expectation to give the world the best of you. The following night she died. I had a decision to either quit and succumb to the pain of living without her or pick up and keep going to become the best person I could be in her honor. She was my why.

While she was it for me, the question is, what is that one thing that is keeping you focused, grounded, and pushing harder than you ever could to reach your full potential? Is it the small voice inside you, your family, or your want for a better life? I need you to grab onto that, grit your teeth and keep going on your journey.

There are so many people depending on you, and while this journey isn't easy, it's required to produce all of what you have to unleash to help the world evolve. I know some days it seems like your goals are out of reach, and there's still a long road ahead of you, but persist.

Each step, small win, and milestone creates momentum thrusting you to manifest your goals quicker. You are closer to reaching your goals because you had the courage to start. The resistance you've undergone, the setbacks, and the failures were just testing your faith to ensure that you're committed to your future self.

Even though it may be hard to see it, realize that we need you. Your family, friends, people in the grocery stores, on the highways, strangers across the world, and the millions of lives that you haven't even touched yet need you. And you ask why? Because, there will never be another like you. Nobody that talks like you, influences, looks, creates, and exists like you.

We need you to fight from within to win the battle that exists outside. You have been molded to take on everything that is in front of you by just being yourself.

I challenge you to create a legacy for your loved ones and to leave an imprint in this world. Choose to live and fulfill everything that you were created to share. Pick the path that feels like it's an uphill battle. This path may be hard but is guaranteed to enrich the lives of others because of your presence on this earth.

Jori Mundy

Award-Winning International Keynote Speaker, Executive, Author, Upcoming TEDx Speaker, Life and Career Coach Jori Mundy has had her fair share of setbacks, triumphs, losses, and gains in her lifetime.

Dedicated to serving and inspiring people as a public servant, life and career coach, she has helped individuals reach their personal and professional goals. On stage, she is known for captivating her audiences with edge-of-the-seat story-telling. She is a past Board member of the Executive Women in Texas Government Organization. She is a 2019 graduate of the National Leadership America program. She is a four-time first-place award-winning International speech contest winner. In 2020, she was featured in The Evolving Woman e-magazine. She has spoken on a variety of platforms for varying organizations to both large and small audiences. To learn more about Jori, you can visit her website Jorimundy.com and on various social media platforms.

Inspirational Message by
Nadine Owens

"When life problems, setbacks, and situations knock you down but didn't knock you out. Yet, you choose to stand."

NADINE OWENS

One thing that I can say about life is that it is unpredictable, uncertain, unsure about problems, setbacks, and situations that we are facing day to day. You cannot change what happened to you, but you can change how you react and respond. My name is Nadine Owens, and I am the certified life coach, international motivational speaker, best-selling author, advocate for families for people with different abilities, and I am the voice of hope. Raising my adult sons with autism took a toll on me mentally and physically. I was depressed for over 20 years. I suffered from anxiety, low self-esteem, and I was stuck and didn't know how to get out of the life cycle I was in. Nothing changed until I decided that I wanted to live.

I wanted to unleash what was inside of me for a greater impact. First, I wanted to start off by telling you that it is possible. All things are possible to them that believe. You have to believe in yourself because if you don't, then who will? You must change your mindset and make a shift in the limited belief that you've been telling yourself. "You can do all things through Christ which strengthens you" (Philippines 4: 13), but until you recognize your true worth and learn how to embrace your uniqueness, you won't be able to achieve the things you're fighting for.

Start the process and knowledge that you possess the creativity, and you can achieve anything you put your mind upon. So, remember, trouble doesn't always last. You have what it takes to push through any obstacle that will grow you and can lead to more opportunities.

Be the Best Version of Yourself

Continue learning, growing, and challenging yourself. Constantly learning is a lifelong process. Every day you can learn something new, to be better than you were yesterday. Always start with the end in mind. Where do you want to see yourself in 6 to 12 months? Prioritize, choose to be happy, don't waste your time on people, places, and things that are not adding value to your life. Your time is important, and it is essential that you delegate it effectively.

Loving Yourself

Learning how to fall in love with yourself is essential for one's happiness, your relationship, and the view of oneself. When you fall in love with yourself, the love will spread quickly, improving the life to others around you. You will not only produce who you are, but you will attract who you are. Establish positive thinking. Get a tribe of people that are focused, loving, and that have the same mission as you. You are doing something meaningful and bringing satisfaction.

To unleash your undeniable impact, you must bring mind, body, and spirit into balance. Maintaining balance can be challenging but is necessary to create overall well-being. Finding a balance between rest and activity creates an emotional, mental, and physical balance to keep yourself motivated and refuel.

Nadine Owens

Nadine-Pritchard Owens is the CEO of Our Brother's Keeper, INC, also known as OBK. Nadine has been a caregiver and parent advocate for more than 20 years to her adult sons with different abilities. She knows firsthand the challenges, the struggles, and the emotional rollercoaster that goes hand and hand with pouring out so much. Nadine is a Certified Life Coach, financial advisor, administrator, author, international motivational speaker, and certified emotional intelligence coach.

Nadine consults with women, men, and people with different abilities. Nadine has a feeding program, and she also trains parents on how to handle stress in a healthy manner. Nadine believes in the biblical principles which shaped and formed her into the woman she is today. www.ourbrotherskeeper.org

Kisma Panthier-Jn Pierre

"The future belongs to those who believe
in the beauty of their dreams."

ATTRIBUTED TO ELEANOR ROOSEVELT

To a tiny ten-year-old girl who had experienced a little bit too much for her age already, a better future was the only tangible thing she had to hold on to for some comfort.

On this beautiful, sunshiny day in the schoolyard of this small Caribbean island, she stood for a few moments looking up in the distance just over the crimson-red crown of the blossoming flamboyant tree just outside her grade six classroom. Like a painter, she used that picture as the inspiration for what her painting would be birthed out of. And as if being guided by some divine inspiration, this otherwise sad, lonely, forsaken, and broken little girl created a masterpiece of her future life, stage by stage, year by year, and moment by moment. Her vision board was not written on paper. It was painted on her heart and in her mind. Her future was born. Her better life was created. And her life was never going to be the same again.

Do you remember that day when you were ten or eleven or twelve when you created the life you wanted to live? You saw the vision that would have created a successful life for you? That would make you happy? What happened to that dream? Did you allow life to take over your dream, and then you stopped living? Are you merely surviving at this moment? I encourage you to wake up out of the nightmare you are living in and go back to dreaming about that beautiful future you created before you let life with all of its cares take over.

One day when she was much older, that little girl stopped to take stock of how much she had accomplished. She was so excited to learn that she had achieved every one of those goals that she had laid out when she was just ten years old. Things had worked out nearly exactly like she had set out in that blueprint on that sunny day.

But guess what she realized? Life had come to a standstill after the 30-year mark. She had stopped dreaming. Like you, this girl, now a woman, had gotten lost in the workings of life, taking care of everybody but herself, making sure that everybody else was encouraged to pursue their dreams. But there was no one to do that for her, no one to push her, to encourage her, to tell her that she still has it in her.

I am that someone. I am here to tell you that you still have it in you. It is still a sunshiny day. You are still the architect of your life. You are the master. If you will believe it strong enough, if you want it badly enough, if you will simply start dreaming again, like me, you will get up out of your nightmare and chase your dreams! Now, go and be all that you are destined to be!

Kisma Panthier-Jn Pierre

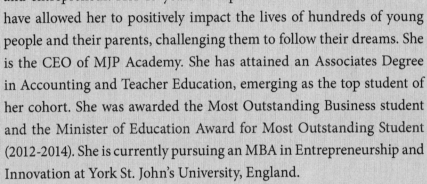

Kisma Panthier-Jn Pierre, alias Madame Jn Pierre, is a passionate French teacher and entrepreneur. Her 15 years of experience have allowed her to positively impact the lives of hundreds of young people and their parents, challenging them to follow their dreams. She is the CEO of MJP Academy. She has attained an Associates Degree in Accounting and Teacher Education, emerging as the top student of her cohort. She was awarded the Most Outstanding Business student and the Minister of Education Award for Most Outstanding Student (2012-2014). She is currently pursuing an MBA in Entrepreneurship and Innovation at York St. John's University, England.

Her humble beginnings, fueled by a determination to make a positive impact with her story, have brought her to this pivotal moment in her career. Kisma lives with her husband on the Caribbean island of Antigua & Barbuda. Learn more about Kisma at www.mjnpacademy.com and connect on social media @kismaJnpierre.

Inspirational Message by
Rita Pilate

"He who believes in Me, the works that I do he will do also, and greater works than these he will do."

JESUS CHRIST

Whatever your faith, there's no denying the immeasurable impact of Jesus Christ on the world. Yet He tells us that believers will do Greater Works???!!!

"Who me??? Yes! You and me!" As believers, we can impact the world and do great works with a simple strategy:

I Intentional
M Moments
P Power
A Action
C Create
T Transformation

I.M.P.A.C.T.™ - INTENTIONAL MOMENTS POWER ACTION CREATE TRANSFORMATION

Have you ever heard an award ceremony speaker credit their success to a moment early in life with a parent, teacher, or counselor? Those moments sparked a transformation in their life.

A catalyst can be defined as a person that precipitates an event. The Jesus within us is our own internal catalyst and makes us a catalyst for others. When we accept our role, we impact the lives of everyone we encounter. Seemingly insignificant moments can change hearts, minds, and lives. Just like water over time shapes even the hardest rocks, small moments shape lives and our world.

"OK, I'm down for that. I can do small moments. *But greater works than these? Jesus performed miracles!*" I'm reminded of the story by Loren Eiseley about the boy walking on the beach picking up starfish and intently throwing them into the ocean so they can live. A man said to him, "There must be millions of stranded starfish! You'll never make a difference." The boy replied, " I made a difference for that one." A tiny fraction of millions, but lifesaving for the one! One starfish's miracle.

The boy was using the talent given him to do what he was called to do. To save millions may seem an impossible feat, yet he committed to transforming the fate of those starfish one by one. Now, what if the man was inspired to help? What if the crowd on that beach joined in? What if it was posted online and people on beaches around the world were also inspired? A catalyst unleashes Miracle upon Miracle; Starfish World is transformed!

Some are called to serve the masses – maybe on stage, on screen, or via a pen. If this is you, answer the call. *Don't be like me, thinking, "It can't be me. This must be for someone else to deliver."* There are no mistakes. It's for you. No matter how improbable it seems. Your message may create that Miracle moment someone needs to unleash their I.M.P.A.C.T.™.

One last thing … a chemical catalyst increases the rate of reaction *without* being consumed. Givers often have many people they love or causes they believe in. We juggle multiple balls. If they all collide, the results are devastating! No matter the cause or how much you love someone, *DON'T* be consumed. My challenge to you … Be a CATALYST and UNLEASH YOUR I.M.P.A.C.T.™!

Rita Pilate

Rita Pilate is the C.E.O. of Profits Plus Coaching LLC, a global network of coaches and experts that helps executives, professionals, small business owners, and entrepreneurs to achieve transformational results. Rita specializes in executive and success coaching. She leverages her 20 plus years of corporate experience at Fortune 100 companies to empower and equip leaders to grow their business and improve their ROI. She is also an expert training facilitator. Rita helps leaders to discover their superpowers so they can live their best life now and create a lasting legacy of success. Rita holds a BS in Chemical Engineering from Howard University and an MS in Chemical Engineering from the University of Florida. She's an avid reader, a lifelong lover of learning, and an author.

Rita Pilate
www.ritapilate.com
Connect with Me on LinkedIn

Inspirational Message by
Tanya D. Powell

"You are a real-life miracle and a living breathing force for good. And the power has always been inside of you to believe - not only in yourself but also in the power of your wildest dreams."

JAMIE KERN LIMA

Have you ever found yourself in a place of knowing that there is more to life for you, but you feel stuck, overwhelmed, perhaps even doubtful or fearful?

I've been there, and I know that too often, we forget how powerful we are. We forget our purpose and passion as life happens. Sometimes our self-image gets crushed, and we start to doubt our abilities, self-worth, and value.

But, here's what I know about you, YOU are a powerful, creative being, capable of BEING, DOING, and HAVING more of what life has to offer. You were made in the image of God to do amazing things and to create an undeniable impact in this world. And the truth is, your world needs you. Your world is waiting on you. Someone is waiting for you to *Unleash Your Undeniable Impact.*

I wasn't so sure that this related to me as I was content playing small in my job, giving as much service as I felt I could. Or so I thought. Yes, I was climbing the corporate success ladder, but I knew deep down something was missing. I was not feeling fulfilled. I was not living my purpose. As I looked around, I saw that many of us had lost our voice, had subdued our light, had lost our passion.

Now, we've all had times of distractions in our lives that threaten to derail us from our destiny. My moment was in 2019 when I was diagnosed with breast cancer. And at that moment, I had to decide WHO I wanted to be and how I wanted to show up for the rest of my life.

"Your life will meet you exactly where your mind is." – Lisa Nichols

You see, I realized that I, too, had a voice and now an incredible message to share with the world. A message that we can Grow and Thrive through adversity and not just go through it and survive! A major mindset shift!

As you find yourself in a test, what is that testimony, or if it's quite a mess, what's the message? Dr. Cheryl Wood says it best, 'your story is about you, but it ain't for you.' It is time to bring YOU to the front of the room because your voice matters.

Take these three steps and tap into your Personal Power and choose you:

1. Decide what you truly want. Create that vision and give it everything you've got. Visualize it every day.
2. Believe that it is done. Remind yourself of who you are and the power within you. Find that greatness within you.
3. Become that version of yourself. Master your self-image and step out with courage and faith. Align your actions with your vision.

Your playing small is denying the world, so answer the call. It's your call, not a group conference or zoom call. Your life is a blueprint for someone's success. So, make the choice today to step up, step out and ***Unleash your Undeniable Impact!***

Tanya D. Powell

Tanya is an International Speaker, #1 Best-Selling Author, and a Results Coach. She empowers individuals to transform their leadership skills to create success in their personal and professional lives. Tanya strongly believes that lasting results are created by transforming from the inside out and effectively guides her clients and audiences to create powerful mindset shifts that elevate them from where they are to where they long to be.

Tanya has spent over two decades in Multibillion-Dollar companies serving in Senior Leadership positions. She is now a Certified Executive and Personal Development Coach with John Maxwell Team and the CAPP Institute. She is an International Award-winning Team engagement coach. Tanya has been a featured speaker on international stages with speakers such as Les Brown, Jon Talarico, and Dr. Cheryl Wood. Known as 'The People's Coach,' Tanya believes that *"It is in change that you discover your purpose."*

Connect: TanyadPowell.com; @tanyadpowell1

Inspirational Message by
Monica D. Reed

"Before I formed you in the womb I knew you; Before you were born I sanctified you; I ordained you a prophet to the nations."

JEREMIAH 1:5 (NKJV)

*Y*ou were born to IMPACT this world. You may be delayed, but you have not been denied by GOD. The world is waiting on YOU to stop denying them access to your solution and for you to Unleash Your VOICE.

The first time I stood before a crowd to share my story was the most memorable moment of my life. There I was trying to gain clarity around my overall life mission; I shared my marital journey. I shared in front of the crowd how I felt that my life had no real significance. After graduating high school, I immediately became a mom, a wife with no other goal but to be the best mom and wife.

After ten minutes of sharing my journey that my husband and I had overcome many challenges as "two young kids raising kids" and being married for over 15 years, my now mentor stopped me to say, "THAT is what the world needs to hear."

Immediately we took a break during this life-changing event. I then proceeded to the restroom, where I found a line full of women who were once in my shoes waiting to get advice from who...yes...ME!

From that moment forward, the way that I viewed my journey in life immediately changed.

"The two most important days of your life are the day you were born and the day you find out why" – The Apocryphal Twain

After that moment, I went on to write my first book. Those women were waiting for a solution through their challenges. Just to think….I had it.

Never would I doubt my journey again. While it was hard to understand why I had to go through all the pain of the journey, I finally knew what to say and who to help with my story. I just knew that it was time to take action. Show up, speak, teach and reach those who were assigned to my life, my voice, my story.

10 Steps to Your Undeniable Impact

1. Understand who created you and who you are.
2. Never allow those who can't handle the authentic you to stop you from using your voice.
3. Don't doubt the assignment that God has given to you.
4. Elaborate on the lessons learned on your journey.
5. Now is the time for you to share your story.
6. Impact only takes place after you take action.
7. Allow others to borrow the same strength that was granted to you by God.
8. Beware of the distractions (people, places, and things) that can be fatal to your destiny.
9. Learn how to position yourself as an authority in your community.
10. Execute Your Assignment and Unleash your Undeniable IMPACT on the world NOW!

Keep in mind that God didn't bring you through all of that for you to keep it to yourself!

Key Takeaway: YOUR journey was HIS plan!

It's Time to Unleash Your Undeniable IMPACT

Unleash Your VOICE to Speak, Teach & Reach the World

7 Steps to Identifying Your Ultimate Life Purpose
www.HERjourneyHISplan.com

Monica D. Reed

Monica D. Reed was born to impact the nation. She has been on a mission to change the world, one woman at a time. Monica is a mother of four beautiful and amazing children. Monica is an award-winning, 11x #1 International Best-Selling Author, Transformational Speaker, and Business Consultant.

Monica started her journey as an entrepreneur by sharing her marital journey with the world in her first book leading to building healthy marriages and women empowerment communities. In 2017, Monica launched her coaching, then speaking career helping purpose-driven women find their voices to reach back and pull another woman up. Monica continues to make significant marks on her legacy by changing the trajectory for several family generations to follow. **HER Impact & Success Academy** helps speakers, leaders, and consultants to take their businesses to the next level and is marked as the FIRST Black-owned entrepreneur business center of Bucks County, PA.

Email: contact@herbusinesscenter.com

Inspirational Message by
Netasha B. Reed

"All that I wanted to become I became; therefore I am."

STORMY WELLINGTON

I stand before you a successful, profitable business owner, Author, and business profits coach. I am all these things and more because I first had to tell myself I am. "Thoughts become things." (Bob Proctor) Now, this was not always the case. What if I told you that based on statistics, I should not be the person that sits here today writing in this book? I had my first child at thirteen years old, and by the time I was twenty-one, I had all five of my children. Some would be ok with living with the bare minimum. Not me. My struggles made me determined to be all that I could be so my kids would not have to not live life in poverty due to my mishaps.

I received my G.E.D, which means I dropped out of high school. I was always very smart and acted grown (as my granny would say), so my mother always allowed me to do what I wanted. So, if I did not get up and go to school, nobody made me. I later went to trade school for Medical Assisting and graduated with the highest honors. After graduation, I went straight into entrepreneurship. I loved being my own boss and creating opportunities for other people. Though I wanted to be a boss running a business with little formal experience, the money was tight and went back into the business, so I ended up getting a nursing job and became a part-time boss lol. I worked in nursing for ten years. My salary was capped, and when I hurt my back, I was replaced. (My blessing) I was already working with my entertainment company and my printing company, so now I could go back to my passion full time. Now, this was no easy task, but I knew that I had so much more to give. I decided to give my businesses my all, just like I had done for my former employers when I traded hours for dollars. I would never be late for work. I stayed late and even worked from home if I had to. I started doing the same for my own business putting in 16–18-hour days. I knew my business would be successful and profitable. In addition to working on my business, I worked on myself. I listened to personal development tapes on Mindset and manifesting, and I took massive action immediately. I knew that if it was meant to be, it was up to me. I took the focus off generating money and focused on helping as many people as possible that needed my services. I also focused on employing those that really wanted to work and saw my vision. One rule I learned was the more people you help make money, the more money you will make. I will leave you with this. Man is made or unmade by their daily choices. Choose your future daily. "Man is the maker of himself." (James Allen)

Netasha B. Reed

Netasha B. Reed is a serial entrepreneur acclaimed for her epic roles in Business Management, Promotions, and Entertainment. Netasha discovered at an early age that to live the life she wanted, she would have to be her own Boss. Netasha was self-inspired with a desire to be very wealthy and help others do the same.

Netasha B. Reed is an Author and Speaker, Business Coach, Health and Wellness Advocate. The Founder of Jazzy Lady Printing (Texas), Jazzy Lady Printing (Georgia), Jazzy Lady Management & Promotions, Maximum Tax Pros and Consulting (4 Locations Texas and Georgia). Netasha uses her proven I.M.D. Method to Inspire, Motivate and Demonstrate (I.M.D) the success of a serial entrepreneur. Netasha now teaches her renowned I.M.D. business model through her course (Gettingtotheprofits.com). Her success and failures are an example of how your mindset can change everything. For more information about me, please visit www.netashabreed.com

Inspirational Message by
La Tina Regan

"...real quality of life is determined by what you do in less-than-optimal situations and the way you fare under pain and pressure."

I.V. HILLIARD

*L*et's face it, most of us are not exempt from hardships or handicaps. Though, how you decide to handle life challenges can impact the outcome. You see, you were designed to thrive; it is in your DNA. Do you need proof? Well, take a moment to think about the many less-than-optimal situations you have already overcome. While you are reflecting, highlight the strength and strategy that lead to those victorious moments. Now, put the reasons behind the victories on repeat in your mind. Let them serve as evidence that success is inevitable for you when you keep going. "This I recall to my mind, and therefore I have hope" is what the prophet Jeremiah said in the book of Lamentations. Past triumphs breed testimonies that can speak hope to you in a present tribulation. They build confidence in the truth that you are not ordinary but extraordinary, and you can always win with the right outlook, even under pressure. Never underestimate your God-given strength and ability to still live a wonderful, enjoyable, quality life after disappointment, detriments, and setbacks.

Understanding your capacity to succeed is only one segment. After you win, show someone else how to do the same. Individuals who may have encountered similar obstacles can benefit from your lessons. No, you cannot change what has occurred. You can, however, choose to alter your perspective. There is a saying, "when life gives you lemons, make lemonade and then sell it." Here is your opportunity. Turn those painful moments into a pathway to empower people. Unleash your undeniable impact on the lives of others with confidence. You have the experience to be a hero of hope. Yes, it can be intimidating or even embarrassing to share former, personal struggles. I definitely would say to exercise wisdom but not withhold the knowledge that could influence a constructive outcome for another in need. One way to truly have a quality life is by creating footprints the next generation can follow. Be inspired to make a difference.

La Tina Regan

La Tina Regan, a business development expert, is a highly regarded influencer and inspirational speaker. She works with local leaders, artists, entrepreneurs, SVP and CEO, youth groups, and nonprofit organizations. She specializes in event solutions and assisting nonprofit organizations. She is also the Senior Pastor of Cornerstone Family Worship Church, Las Vegas NV; www.cornerstonefwc.org. Booking information: latina.regan@gmail.com.

Inspirational Message by

Anthony D. Shannon, Sr

"Roll your works upon the Lord [commit and trust them wholly to Him; He will cause your thoughts to become agreeable to His will, and] so shall your plans be established and succeed."

PROVERBS 16:3 (AMP)

"If we let our desires lead our decisions, our lives (and our bodies) can quickly spin out of control. Self-control is a discipline that God grows in us when we continually choose to die to our flesh and live in Him."

GALATIANS 5:22-23

THE PRICE TAG OF LEADERSHIP IS "SELF-DISCIPLINE"

You must ask yourself. Are you willing to do the work that is required to get you there?

It is not what you are that holds you back; it is what you think you are not. That is what holds you back.

*You cannot always control circumstances, but you can change your thoughts and add discipline, but nothing changes until your Mind Changes.

What is your Biggest Problem in Leadership? IT'S LEADING yourself.

It's much easier to lead yourself because it's easier to teach what you know but living it is hard. It takes Intentional Living. I am convinced that everyone wants to have success.

(See People are preparing or repairing. See 70% of all people getting fired are relationship issues)

WISDOM KEY: Self-discipline is what allows you and me to get better. Here's how it works. In the beginning, you are not as bad as people say you are, but if you start out good, then over time, you will be as good as people think you are. It's called Consistency!

I have found out that truly Everything Worthwhile Is UPHILL. Nothing in life comes easy or quick; it's all an UPHILL battle, and it takes discipline. Even scriptures bear us out that we must fight to stay believing, and here is what it says.

"Fight the good fight of the faith; lay hold of the eternal life to which you were summoned and [for which] you confessed the good confession [of faith] before many witnesses." 1 Timothy 6:12 (AMP)

YOU must fight for your dreams every day. You must climb for your dreams every day – It doesn't come to you, and it's not in 3 easy packages, and it doesn't come overnight. All my life, I worked hard to become an Overnight Success. Everything worthwhile is UPHILL.

Wisdom Key > If you have Downhill Habits and UPHILL HOPES, you are in trouble, and the only way you go uphill is SELF-DISCIPLINE.

IT IS IMPOSSIBLE TO HAVE CONTINUED SUCCESS WITHOUT SELF-DISCIPLINE. MY GREATEST CHALLENGE AS A LEADER every day IS KEEPING PEOPLE CLIMBING because they don't want to climb; they want to coast to success. There is no straight line for success. Let's investigate the book of Wisdom.

The LORD does not let the righteous go hungry, but He denies the craving of the wicked. Idle hands make one poor, but diligent hands bring wealth. He who gathers in summer is a wise son. We see that even the Lord does not just give you what you want, but it takes hard work.

Anthony D. Shannon, Sr

Anthony D. Shannon, Sr AKA SPEAKER-T is a Thought-Provoking leader in the Corporate World and now in the motivational speaking and training industry. He is an American author, speaker, and Pastor who has written two books and produced 4 Manuals, primarily focusing on leadership. Anthony was born in Pontiac, Michigan, and is an evangelical Christian. He followed his Mother into the ministry. He completed a bachelor's degree at Southern Christian University in 1988 and a Master of Divinity degree at Southern Christian University. Shannon is a leadership expert, speaker, and author in the areas of corporate leadership, Casting vision, time-management, consultative B2B sales, business development, and coaching. He has impacted countless lives across the United States, helping individuals realize that change is necessary for their personal and business growth and know that Overing to Win is always possible even when the odds are stacked up against you. Shannon has a unique ability to be pedagogy and didactic, engaging, motivating, and inspiring leaders of all levels to achieve their vision. Twenty-five years of Corporate experience from Sales Training to District Vice President and Vice President positions with Companies like ADP, CERDIAN, MARRIOTT, TOTAL SOURCE, STAFFPLUS, and PAYCHEX, Shannon has also been responsible for overseeing the success of training departments with over 3000 employees. During that time, Shannon has created and delivered world-class award-winning presentations on large stages within corporations all across the United States and now working on expanding into Canada and other international countries.

Website URL: anthonydshannonconsultinggroup.com

Inspirational Message by
Dr. Onika L. Shirley

"As I walked out the door toward the gate that would lead to my freedom, I knew if I didn't leave my bitterness and hatred behind, I'd still be in prison."

NELSON MANDELA

Give yourself permission to forgive, heal, and live. Each of us has some things we are bearing resentment on. Throughout our lifetime, we sometimes resent situations, and sometimes we resent people, but each of us has the choice of forgiveness. It can be a new outlook or a healthy distance. I believe one of the most important things you can do to maximize your impact in 2021 and years to come is to be laser-focused on your life's purpose. Things will happen to keep you distracted and try to prevent you from walking in purpose. We don't forgive because we agree, but we do it to be free. Forgiveness frees us, and it builds others up. Forgiveness can connect broken families, build our communities, and change our world. But to have the most impact, it's important to give wisely. Maximize your planned giving by forgiving all and forgiving quickly. Think about your purpose in life. You want to ensure that nothing is hindering you from living it out.

Three Ways to Maximize Your Impact with Forgiveness.

1. Think about your past. What's broken? Commit to fixing it.

2. Collaborate with others. Who's missing? Be the bigger person and extend grace.

3. Focus on reunification. Where's your peace? Are you truly happy?

Forgiveness helps you unleash your undeniable impact in the world by being a better version of yourself. You were the bigger person when you were seen as small, a pushover, or an object of negativity. Think about how much you contribute to the world and your personal impact in it when you forgive a situation or person who tried to bring you down or do you wrong.

Forgive, heal, and live. Unforgiveness has a stronghold in one's life. An unforgiving, vindictive, or bitter spirit will not only affect you and those around you but will also separate you from the blessings of God. The blessings of God are healing. The blessings of God are life. Maximize your impact in the world by acting of the will and not from how you feel and from your emotions. Forgiveness is not a feeling.

In summary, to increase your impact in 2021, keep rising above the obstacles, do the unthinkable, and focus on tripling your efforts in forgiving situations and people that aimed to cause you to be in bondage. Without forgiveness, we end up giving control of our life to the situation or the person who caused the pain. Forgiveness can't be about how they will respond or what they will say or do. Forgiveness for all is about what we do and our undeniable impact in the world. Forgiveness is not about giving up our drive towards purpose. Mother Teresa, Dr. Martin Luther King, and Nelson Mandela never gave up their determination to make the world a better place, regardless of opposition. Their capacity for forgiveness did not weaken their determination to fight for what they knew to be right and their individual impact on the world.

Dr. Onika L. Shirley

Dr. Onika L. Shirley, the Founder and CEO of Action Speaks Volume, Inc., is an International Procrastination Strategist and Behavior Change Expert. She is known for building unshakable confidence, stopping procrastination, and getting your dreams out of your head into your life. She is also a Motivational Speaker and a Christian Counselor.

Dr. Onika is the Founder and Director of Action Speaks Volume Orphanage Home in India, Action Speaks Volume Sewing School in Pakistan, Empowering Eight Inner Circle, P6 Solutions and Consulting, and ASV C.A.R.E.S. She is a bestselling author, master storyteller, and serial entrepreneur. Dr. Onika is a biological mother, adoptive mother, foster mother, and proud grandmother to baby Aubrey and little Kendalynn. Of all the things Dr. Onika does, she is most proud of her profound faith in Christ and her opportunity to serve the body of Christ globally. Dr. Onika walks with a purpose.

CoWano Ms. Coco Stanley

"......With confidence you have won before you have started."

MARCUS GARVEY

*I*n life, you dream or visualize to have the ability and skills to do what is needed to be comfortable and happy. But dreaming or visualizing life does throw some curveballs and obstacles in your path. What do you do when this happens? Do you have the confidence and faith to keep moving forward, or do you stay stuck and defeated? Well, let me tell you this, every area of your life will consist of having confidence and faith to accomplish tasks and goals that you want. Your confidence plays a major part in your life. Having confidence will take you further than someone who doesn't believe in him or herself. When you begin to find yourself with low confidence (or low self-esteem), find the courage from within and pull yourself up and get your confidence back. Depending on how low your confidence is, it may feel a little challenging at first but don't give up. You must find some tools that will help you walk in confidence daily. One of the best tools is meditation and affirmations daily. You need to have the confidence to be the best parent, to be the best employee, to be the best at your talent/skill, to be the best at speaking, to be the best at running a business, to be the best student, to be the best author and more. Do not let life obstacles, challenges, and circumstances stop you from having the confidence to keep moving forward and accomplishing your goals. You must believe in yourself more than anyone else. When I had a child at the age of 20, I had no idea what kind of parent I would turn out to be. But I honestly believe no matter what came my way, I would push through and be the best mother I could be. I truly had that confidence in me. See, when you have confidence, you walk in it. You feel it and are self-assured about who you are. When walking in confidence, you have the boldness to go after the things in life that others will not. When you walk in confidence, you are up for the challenges that may come your way. Confidence is one of the keys to the doors that you are seeking for God to open. You are here for a purpose to be a blessing to someone. If you allow life situations or circumstances to put you in a place of not believing in yourself, then you cannot be that blessing to others. Yes, we must go through some life lessons but do not let them keep you stuck and fearful. You are in control of your mind and the thoughts that go in and out. So, make sure you have self-care of yourself every day to have the confidence to conquer each day. Make sure you have the confidence to go out there and accomplish all that you need and desire. You can do it.

CoWano Ms. Coco Stanley

CoWano Ms. Coco Stanley is from El Dorado, AR, but she grew up in Minneapolis, MN. One of the most significant events in her life was the birth of her son. At that time, she was 20 years old. As a single parent, she was still able to complete two Master's degrees. While raising her son, she went through some tough times. However, she began to experience a lack of confidence within herself due to several abusive relationships. She learned how to overcome a crisis of confidence and regain her confidence back. CoWano walked away from the corporate world in 2018. She started her own cleaning business, became an author, and started her coaching program. Her passion is to show other women how to get their confidence back. CoWano's mission is to provide women with support and tools to walk in confidence to a path of starting their business.

Inspirational Message by
Roni Benjamin-Talley

"Live Full, Die Empty"
LES BROWN

*I*f today was the last day of your life, can you say you lived full out? My biggest fear is getting to the end of my life with regrets about how I lived, wasted gifts, skills, ideas, and talents that God gave me. Les Brown said, "The graveyard is the richest place on earth because it's where you'll find all of the hopes and dreams that were never fulfilled, books that were never written, songs never sung, inventions never shared, and cures never discovered." I looked back over my life and noticed several times where I was excited about a new endeavor, and I let fear, self-doubt, and other people's opinion dictate whether I would move forward or not. Doing the same thing over and over, expecting a different result, is the definition of insanity. I wanted different results so bad that I was willing to take massive disruptive action. I embarked on a difficult journey of self-discovery. I had to face the trauma from my past that had taken root in my subconscious and deterred me from living the life I was purposed to live. The trauma of sexual molestation at age six by a stranger and again at age eight by someone I loved dearly. You can imagine how confused I was dealing with experiences adults couldn't even handle. With no counseling nor the communication skills to express myself, I went through life like so many others carrying the weight of trauma unresolved.

I am sure you can attest that unresolved trauma from the past will sprout up in other areas of your life. Remnants of my trauma sprouted in my teenage years as I filled the void of self-love by accepting a 'side chick' role which later led to me being a young mother at age 20. Traces of my trauma sprouted again in my young adult years as I ran into the arms of broken men who physically and mentally broke me down to the core. I had every justified reason to point fingers at everyone who hurt me and disappointed me over my lifetime. Yet, I chose to take ownership of my life and participate in my own rescue.

I hired a counselor and life coach to help me overcome past trauma. Most importantly, I made an unwavering commitment to myself. I read books and listened to audios from Les Brown, Lisa Nichols, and others who reminded me that I have greatness within me and that I have the birthright to live full and die empty. I surrounded myself with who I call "Love Mirrors." They looked at me and saw brilliance, beauty, and qualities that I could not see at first. I simply borrowed their belief in me until I truly believed them when I looked at myself in the mirror. I did the work. You, too, can do the work by downloading the exercises that helped me break through trauma and live up to my fullest potential at roniuplifts.com.

Roni Benjamin-Talley

Roni Benjamin-Talley was born and raised in Queens, NYC Astoria Housing Projects. Despite her humble beginning, Roni embraced her inner superhero and started her own business. As a licensed financial professional, Roni commits her voice to fighting in the war of economic inequality and financial literacy. She wears her armor every day and prepares for battle one conversation at a time. In addition to running a successful business, she is an Artist, in which she showcased her talent as a cast member of multiple award-winning stage plays. Adding to her resume, she entered the journey of public speaking in which she co-hosted radio shows and delivers motivational talks throughout the country. As a bestselling author, Roni understands the power of using words to uplift and inspire others to move into action.

Connect with Roni
Instagram @ RoniUplifts
Facebook Roni M Benjamin
ronibenjamin.com

Inspirational Message by
Melanese Marr-Thomas

"You can't do anything about the length of your life, but you can do something about its width and depth."

SHIRA TEHRANI

We are all given 86,400 seconds each day. Often, we take for granted those 86,400 seconds because we believe another day will magically appear. It appeared yesterday, so why would it not appear tomorrow? However, no one knows the exact number of days we are allotted to live. Many people go to sleep believing they would see tomorrow, only not to open their eyes to their next 86,400 seconds.

On February 28, 2021, my dear husband never received his complete 86,400 seconds. At 10 PM, my husband took his last breath, believing he had more time. He was scheduled to work the next morning. We had plans to celebrate our 10th wedding anniversary in Jamaica. Clothes for a photoshoot were purchased. Matching outfits were obtained. Hotel and flights were reserved. Passports were ready for new stamps. However, none of those plans came to pass.

So often, we just exist. We are doing just the bare minimum to survive. We get up, eat, commute to work, complete our work, commute home, pay bills, participate in a little entertainment, handle family obligations, and go to bed, just to do it all again the next day.

However, to "live," asks us to do and be a lot more. "Living" requires that we move and function on purpose. "Living" requires that we question if we are contributing to the community through acts of service. "Living" requires that we walk in our calling.

We cannot control the length of our life, but we can control how we choose to live. We cannot control the weather, but we can control what we wear or the protection we use on a rainy day. So, instead of living without purpose or disregard for the gift of life, let us begin to focus on the width and depth of life.

Living a wide and deep life seems similar. However, they are not.

Width is the quality of life and includes a wide range of activities, such as our vocation, hobbies, acts of service, and education. Living wide includes all the things we say "yes" to and all the things we say "no" to. Living wide means staying in the moment and allowing life to unfold.

Depth is purpose and meaning in life. It is where we spend our time. It also reflects our priorities and values. Intention is at the center of a deep life. It is working to protect the deep instead of allowing the shallow to control our time, energy, and effort.

What will be the width and depth of your life? Will it be a legacy of love and service? Or a legacy of bitterness, resentment, and unforgiveness? Will your legacy bring joy to your family? Will your children carry your legacy with honor and pride? Or will your legacy be a heavy burden they run away from for the rest of their lives? May God grant you the discernment and peace to pursue BIG GOD-GIVEN dreams. Decide today to live on purpose.

Melanese Marr-Thomas

Melanese Marr-Thomas is an entrepreneur, passionate cook, dream assistant,
consistent encourager, and mother of six. She
is the co-founder, owner and head chef of Sõl Familiá Mobile Kitchen,
a Temple Hills, MD food truck and catering business started with her
late husband, Charles. Due to the untimely passing of her husband, a
new purpose and passion surfaced. Melanese is now a certified widow's
support coach assisting women facing the toughest journey of their life
with hope, grace, and tenacity. She seeks to give space to women as they
walk through their grief journey and assist them in creating their individual and very personal "hope plan" to navigate their new reality and
norm. In addition, Melanese is also a Corporate Recruiter for a small
government contracting firm after serving as a Department of Defense
government contractor for over 15 years.

Website: https://melanesemarr.com
FB: @cookingwithmelanese and @solfamiliamobilekitchen
IG: @cookingwithmelanese and @solfamiliamobilekitchen

Michelle S. Thomas

"Only a man who knows what it is like to be defeated can reach down to the bottom of his soul and come up with the extra ounce of power it takes to win..."

MUHAMMAD ALI

December 12, 2001, my manager announced that I was being laid off! I was a single mother with three amazing sons, all under the age of 11. My bills barely could be kept up WITH the job, "NOW WHAT?!?!" Embarrassed, hurt, hopeless, and defeated, I made it to my car, and as the tears rushed down my face, I screamed, "I GIVE UP GOD!!!" You see, the past few years had been nothing but pain. Within three years, I had had a baby, found my husband cheating, been attacked, tried to commit suicide, filed bankruptcy, was forced to move, gotten divorced, and was starting OVER! The only good thing I thought I had was my JOB… and now that was gone TOO!

I got to the daycare to pick up my two-year-old, trying to avoid the director. I grabbed my kid and ran out before she could ask me about the payments. I was exhausted, and there was not any food at the house. I went to McDonald's and bought three $.50 hamburgers and two $.99 fries. I only had $4.00 in my wallet and had no clue what I would do for the rest of the week, let alone the month. I put the three hamburgers down on the table and split the two fries between the boys. As I was walking away, my oldest asked, "Mommy, where is your food?" Facing away from him, I replied, "Mommy is on a diet, honey!" and rushed into my bathroom and locked the door. I sat in my dry tub for hours crying, too embarrassed to face my own kids. Shamefully I waited until the boys fell asleep before I cowardly came out. On the table was a portion of my oldest's burger on a napkin with about five fries on it with a note saying, "I think I'm on a diet too, mommy!"

I am telling that story because, at the time, all hope was gone for me. I was broke and broken, believing that things could never get better for me. But God had another plan! He knew that my purpose had not been filled. Seeing my young son reflect the caring person I'd always strived to be, gave me STRENGTH! For him to share his food with me may seem like a small deal, but it was the fuel I needed to DECIDE that I was WORTH SOMETHING! My boys believed in me, so I NEEDED to believe in myself ALSO! I could not be the "failure" that I felt at that moment. I had to pick myself up and not just make it... but SUCCEED not only for me but for them! Today I pay my STRENGTH FORWARD! I write this chapter for someone who right now feels hopeless and defeated! I am here to tell you that YOU HAVE the "extra ounce of power" not just to WIN but achieve VICTORY over your life! Press on, my friend. Your PURPOSE has not been filled!

Michelle S. Thomas

Michelle S. Thomas, *Your Relationship Surgeon,* is a 4X Internationally Best-Selling Author, Certified Life/Relationship/Business Coach, Motivational, and Multiple business owner. She believes that everyone has the power to "touch" their dreams. Even before she turned her purpose into her profession, she always recognized that real people needed to hear real stories to conquer what really mattered to them. Her own life story has been one of complicated paths at times, but she has never shied away from telling her truth. Through her own transparency, her audiences receive tools to alleviate their pain, inspire their strength, and resurrect their inner drive. *Your Relationship Surgeon* offers relatable content through her books, private coaching, workshops, and keynote speeches designed to elevate your relationship with yourself, your family, and your business. Let's connect at www.michellesthomas.com.

Inspirational Message by
Donald D. Toldson, Sr.

"There is no greater agony than bearing
an untold story inside you."

MAYA ANGELOU

Your life is meant to live beyond its expectancy. It is meant to be so transformational until it amazes you. Your life was created for you to change the world. You are an undeniable masterpiece that cannot be duplicated or replicated. Your life was given to you because no one else can do it like you. It is yours and yours alone. 1 Corinthians 2:9 states, "Eyes have not seen, ears have not heard, nor has it entered into the hearts of man the things which God has prepared for those that love him." You are the undeniable, real deal, #1, best-selling winner, and "It" was given to you. What untold stories are bearing on the inside of you that need to be shared, seen, and experienced with the world?

I was reflecting on a time in my life when a young lady who is very close to my heart was sentenced to one year in federal prison because she made a mistake by listening to someone she believed to be a trusted friend. If you have ever accepted the advice of someone you trusted and they let you down, then you understand.

Her life did not start that way. She was a successful business owner, wife, and mother of three beautiful children, but she made a mistake.

I went to visit this young lady. I told her regardless of how the world has labeled her because of her current situation, she's still valuable. I watched her as tears began to fall from her eyes as she cried out, "What about the shame I have brought to my family, my husband, and my children? I'm going to do better; I'm going to do better!" I told her, "The Lord himself will go before you, and He will not leave you."

Her current situation did not dictate her current possibilities or her future possibilities, and neither will yours. Even if you can't see it for yourself, you are the catalyst that God has created for the world.

That young lady served her time and developed a hunger for success and declared that she would not be denied, and neither will you.

Why? Because you've spent many hours dreaming and looking in the mirror, wondering, "Can I do this?" You deserve this. You know you have the gifts, the skills, the talents, and the abilities. Don't allow the fear of failure to cause you to sit on the sidelines of life. Before you know it, a year has passed, five years have passed, a decade has passed, and you're still wondering, "Can I do this?"

Yes, you can do this. It was created for you. Your life is meant to live beyond its expectancy. It is meant to be so transformational until it amazes you. Your life was created for you to change the world. You are an undeniable masterpiece that cannot be duplicated or replicated. Your life was given to you because no one else can do it like you. It is yours and yours alone.

Donald D. Toldson, Sr.

Donald D. Toldson, Sr. is an international best-selling author, motivational speaker, entrepreneur, founder, and trainer at Speaking 2 Impact and Change and iCan Speak, Write & Lead Youth Training Program. He has a heart for motivating, encouraging, and inspiring others to conquer their fears by courageously sharing their unique voice, story, and expertise. Toldson provides specialized speaker, writing, and leadership training for those ready to share their message with the world.

Toldson has received numerous awards and accolades to include being inducted into the World Book of Greatness 2021, iChange Nations Civility Icon Newcomer of the Year 2021, iChange Nations Community Ambassador Award, and World Civility Presidential Club award. He has been featured on Atlanta Live!®, Afro-tainment Television®, Gospel Vibes®, and numerous other media outlets.

He is the Immediate Past President of Four Corners Toastmasters and current District 84 Area 50 Director of Toastmasters International.

Inspirational Message by
Willie Mae Starr-White

"My son won't suffer the same fate!"

WILLIE MAE STARR-WHITE

"You take so long to talk!" "No one wants to hear you guck all day!" "I don't have all day; go write it down!" "Stop moving your head and mouth like that!!!!" "Not today with that gucking!"

I remember the constant insulting, ridicule, laughing, mocking, and continuous teasing from my family. I was a joke to them. No one took me seriously, nor took the time to listen to me. My family had no patience for my speech disordered-stuttering.

As a transitional verb, stutter means speaking with involuntary disruption or blocking speech by repetition or prolongation of vocal sounds. I had constant gesturing with my hands, repeated movement of my head, trembling lips, and eye-rolling.

It was the kindness and insight of my mentor and High School English teacher, Dr. Gloria Spencer, that put me on the right path. She said to me, *"Even with straight A's and a high GPA, no one will take you seriously in life if you cannot voice your thoughts."* She made me stay after class every day to read books and newspapers aloud. When I entered the workforce and still stuttered and had no self-esteem, my mentor suggested Toastmasters. I attended a meeting and was impressed with the speaker's confidence and because he stuttered. Surprisingly, no one laughed nor teased. Instead, they provided the speaker with patience, support, and respect. I joined that day, April 1, 2007. I worked hard to be an effective communicator. As a result, I have been speaking fluently for 14 years, and I now mentor and help others who want to improve their oral communication.

When my son entered daycare, I noticed he was stuttering. My heart just broke, but I refused for my son to go through my adversity. I worked with his daycare provider, who helped me enroll him in Head Start programs. When he started elementary school, he still stuttered. I worked with his teachers and PCP to create an IEP and enrolled him into the Allegheny Intermediate Unit program and the Child Development Unit at Children's hospital. They tested both of us and observed our interaction together while playing and talking to each other. They trained me to interact with my son to be patient and supportive during his treatment. One of the most enjoyable and effective suggested treatments was singing. A "Barney" cassette tape had my son and I singing during cleaning time, bath time, saying goodnight to all his toys before bedtime **without stuttering**. These programs helped us both with how to control our breathing, speak slower, stop gesturing our hands, head, trembling lips, and blinking eyes.

To support your fluent speaking quest for self-development, it requires five things:

1. Get yourself or your child tested through the school and PCP.
2. Get educational and emotional training for both the child and parent.
3. Have patience with yourself and your child, not constant frustration.
4. Practice reading and singing songs aloud to yourself and your child.
5. I recommend joining a public speaking organization like Toastmasters.

Willie Mae Starr-White

As a suicide survivor, she promises to show you that LIFE is always the answer!! This life has taught her strength, faith, resilience, and bravery.Willie Mae Starr-White, known as the "Smiling Lady," has worked in the business administration, project and information services, facilities management, and records management industry for 25 years. She has learned to develop optimal organizational structures and perform the strategic planning, financial management, and leadership of the Facilities and Engineering Department.She served in the United States Army Reserves for six years.Willie Mae has been an active member of Toastmasters International for 14 years. She is actively the 2021-2022 VP of Membership, Secretary, and Treasurer of several Toastmasters Clubs. She is enthusiastically working through her Motivational Strategies and Leader Development Pathway Programs. Willie Mae pulls her strength from her loving husband, intelligent and handsome son, and empowering and protective brother. Her compassion consists of all her aunt, uncles, nieces, nephews, and family. You can reach her at: williemaestar492@gmail.com or Willie Mae "Angel" White on Facebook.

Inspirational Message by
Dr. Roberta J. Wilburn

"...if each one of us would examine what
we can do within our own personal
sphere of influence with the skills that
God has given us, we can begin to
eradicate many of the challenges we see so
prevalent in our country. Consider
your sphere of influence and provide the greatest
impact where you are with what you have."

DR. ROBERTA J. WILBURN

What is a life well spent?

Is it the number of years we have spent on earth?

Is it our level of education and the number of degrees we have hanging on our wall?

Is it the wealth we have accumulated? The amount of money we have in the bank?

Is it the possessions we have acquired? Clothes? Cars? Or houses?

No! A life well spent is measured by what we did to help others—what we did to make a difference in the world.

What is a life well spent?

Is it simply thinking about what you want and what's best for you?

No! A life well spent is more than that; it is about thinking more of others than you do yourself.

Yet, a life well spent also means caring for yourself so you can care for others. It is living each day with intention, with passion, with purpose.

It is about heeding the calling of God! It is going where He leads! It is about letting Him show you a more excellent way.

What is a life well spent?
It is doing the best that you can with what you have.

It is caring for people. All people. It is respecting human differences. It is advocating for those who cannot advocate for themselves. It is accepting people just as they are. It is helping them to be their best selves. It is fighting for justice when you see injustice being done. It is seeking dignity for all people. It is walking in authenticity and integrity. It is embracing the fact that others have the right to do the same. Trying to live a life well spent isn't easy. And it's not the road for the faint at heart. But it is possible if you set your mind to it. If you can do these things.... Then you can say that you have lived a life well spent, and you will have made an undeniable impact.

We have each been given a sphere of influence. A place and space where we can have a significant impact. In that place are people whose lives you are supposed to touch. No one else can have the same level of impact as you for the people who God has assigned to you. If you fail to step up to use your voice, sing your song, advocate for those you are supposed to serve, then someone may miss the divine message that can help them go to their next level of success. They may remain stagnant, hopeless, and may never become all that they were created to be.

However, if you will heed the call of the moral imperative to reach out to the marginalized, advocate for racial and social justice, take a stand against those things that you know are wrong even though it puts you in a position of discomfort and distress, then you are on the road to living a life well spent. What will you do? Will you take the challenge?

Dr. Roberta J. Wilburn

Dr. Roberta J. Wilburn is an award-winning diversity, equity, and inclusion (DEI) expert, a bestselling author, diversity trainer, cultural coach, and advocate. She works with people to uncover their hidden biases so they can become culturally sensitive advocates and allies promoting cross-cultural understanding. Using her R.E.A.L. DEI Framework, she teaches and encourages others how to embrace cultural differences, disrupt discriminatory practices, and foster collaborative relationships using a faith-based perspective so they can excel in a diverse and inclusive world. She is known as The Culture Connoisseur because of her program "A Cup of Culture and a Taste of Diversity." Dr. Wilburn is also the Interim Chief Diversity Officers/Associate Vice President for DEI at Whitworth University, as well as President and Co-founder of Wilburn & Associates, LLC. She is married to James Wilburn, Jr., and they have three adult children and three grandsons. For more information, contact her at: www.wilburnassociates.org.

Inspirational Message by
Ebony Williams

"The ultimate measure of a man is nothing where he stands in moments of comfort and convenience but where he stands in times of challenge and controversy."

(DR. MLK)

Unleash yourself!! Stop holding yourself hostage!! Stop hiding in the dark, unmask yourself, stop fighting the feeling, and give yourself permission to be great!!! Shower the world with your gifts, your talents, your powers, and greatness. Now is your time to break those chains that have been holding you back! Now is the time to release yourself from bondage!!! There is so much power and strength within you. The world is waiting on you! No one knows your journey or could tell it better than you! Never has the world seen or heard someone as unique as you. It's your story that's unheard. It's your piece to the puzzle that's missing. It's you that's needed. It is your presence, your testimonies. It's your experiences, your voice, your mind, thoughts, your strengths, your profits your loss that are essential. Authority has been given to you! Now is the time to make your undeniable impact!!! You are the intrinsic one!!

Ebony Williams

My name is Ebony Williams. I am a new and emerging speaker with a lot of experience overcoming obstacles, being resilient, and persevering through pain while still starting and sub-stating a business. I am an entrepreneur of 6 years and a parent of 4 children. My Mission is to share my message with the hope it brings comfort, to help inspire, and motivate someone to overcome their struggles..

ig:euniquestrands

Inspirational Message by
Rhonda M. Wood

"Each meeting occurs at the precise moment
for which it was meant. Usually, when it will
have the greatest impact on our lives."

NADIA SCRIEVA

L ike every mother, I dreamed of a life full of love, laughter, and a bright future for my child. But those dreams changed dramatically when my teenage daughter was diagnosed with depression, anxiety, bipolar disorder, and suicidal ideations. As a single mom, my road was already challenging. And my reality was only compounded by the fact that I was working a full-time, high-level corporate job at one of the most influential law firms in the nation. I was shunned at work, abandoned by family, and looked down on at church. Filled with uncertainty about how I would support my family, I decided to take a leave of absence from work to support my daughter's mental health. I could have let this difficult moment dictate my future, but my story is a reminder that God can turn the deepest pain into His perfection.

A few months after taking leave from my job, I was contacted by the National Alliance on Mental Illness of Prince George's County and extended an opportunity to speak on a panel. They wanted me to share my story of supporting a loved one with a mental health condition. At first, I thought they had the wrong person. I had never shared my story publicly. Nonetheless, I agreed. After sharing my story and walking off the stage, I was amazed at how many people came up to share how my story impacted their lives. A single mother was at her wit's end, a career woman ready to resign, and a police officer wanting more education on mental health in the community. I was asked to write an article by a magazine publisher. And an elected official wanted me to speak to his youth group. I knew that I had discovered my passion and my purpose.

Speaking and sharing my story has made me feel so internally fulfilled because I get to help transform lives. I began to aggressively pursue speaking and coaching as a business. I started to receive opportunities to share my message of empowerment on stages, television, talk shows, radio, podcasts, magazines, and the news. Everything happens for a reason. If I had never been made uncomfortable, especially during a challenging time, I never would have been open to embarking on something new. And I would not be where I am today – living in my passion and purpose with no regrets. Remarkably, my daughter followed in my footsteps and now advocates, speaks, and writes about the mental health stigma among teens and young adults.

God uses and recycles our most painful experiences into a better purpose. Perhaps you, like me, find yourself wandering the detours of life. Don't allow your painful moments to hold you hostage and keep you from propelling into your future. Regardless of how lost you feel, you, too, can unleash your undeniable greatness and leave an impact on this world. I hope my message offers hope and encouragement.

Rhonda M. Wood

Rhonda M. Wood is an empowerment speaker, author, and the world's #1 mental health advocate. Her specialty is helping people reclaim their inner power, make peace with their past, and prosper in their purpose so that they are empowered to reach their highest potential personally and spiritually. Rhonda felt led to use her voice and talents to serve others with a level of transparency that resonates in the hearts of people around the world. In a world where people are expected to stay silent about mental health issues and trauma, Rhonda chooses to speak up and shine light and awareness on matters that have stayed in the darkness for far too long. She has developed a deep-rooted passion for helping others reset their value, renew their vision, restore their vocation, and rediscover their voice and is fully committed to her mission to normalize and destigmatize mental health conversations. . Connect with me on social media @RhondaMWood or https://www.rhondamwood.com.

Constance Woulard, RN, MSN

"Forgive your younger self. Believe in your current self. Create your future self."

AUTHOR UNKNOWN

We are taught as young children through mealtime prayers that "God is great" and that "He is good." (Author unknown) Scripture teaches that God created us in His image and that everything that comes from God is good and perfect. Knowing and receiving these teachings, we often underestimate ourselves and our capabilities. We are unable to embrace our true greatness, failing to realize that God has created us for a divine purpose. It is necessary that we seek God's divine guidance and be obedient to His will in order to walk boldly into our purpose and destiny.

Fear of failure, criticism, negativity from our peers, and life experiences shape and mold our psyche and self-esteem. Rejection by peers instills fear within us and feelings of inadequacy. Depending upon our inner strength and faith in ourselves, we may be unable to accept and embrace our true greatness. The lack of discipline and self-control often prevents us from walking boldly and obediently into our purpose. This deficiency causes us to be unfocused and inattentive to the will of God. The mistakes of our past often hinder our successes and progression into our true purpose. Many opportunities for success have been missed.

Know that individual successes have been preordained by the grace of God before birth. Each of us is destined for greatness, as we were created in His image. This affirms that we are unstoppable and able to achieve well above our wildest dreams. Understand and embrace your innermost feelings regarding self-worth and personal beauty. The healing process begins, and the personal metamorphosis occurs. Accentuate the positive and become cognizant of your strong points. Accentuate your strong points, both physical and spiritual, and allow them to ignite your evolution into the successful individual that God has destined you to become.

How is it possible to unleash your undeniable impact? Maturity brings about a change and a difference in our lives. Spiritual maturity is a necessary evil for success. One must get to know God in his fullness and learn to accept and embrace His love for us. Acceptance of God's divine wisdom and power allows us to embrace him in His fullness and understand that we can do all things through Him. Success is evident; failure is not an option.

Release the demons, the pain, and the failures of your past. "Forgive your younger self." (Author unknown) Embrace past failures and mistakes, knowing they have shaped and refined your destiny towards greatness. Seek intimate fellowship with God. Trust His divine power and will. Free your mind and spirit of negativity and feelings of failure and rejection. Unleash your undeniable impact!!

Constance Woulard, RN, MSN

Constance Woulard is a native of Gulfport, Mississippi. In her current role as Divisional Director of Nursing and Utilization Management, she is accountable for nursing practice and quality across her organization, encompassing thirteen sites within the United States. She has a passion for developing leaders and motivating others to be their best. Her noted accomplishments are as follows:

Motivational speaker
Best-selling author
Nursing educator
Long-term care consultant
Dedicated to developing the next generation of leaders

Inspirational Message by

#BrandMaster,
Martina Britt Yelverton

"Procrastination Is An Arrogant Assumption That
God Will Give You Another Chance TOMORROW
To Do What He Told You To Do TODAY!"

BISHOP ROSIE O'NEAL

3 Steps to Go From Unfocused to Unleashed!

1- Unlearn

We ALL have negative behaviors that we don't realize may be stunting our growth. We wake and rest with a preprogrammed beLIEf that we must take time to unlearn. If we do not take this time, we are destined for a repeat departure from our God-given destination. Is there something that you do because you were taught or told to?

I'll use a can opener as an example. I was taught to turn the can opener on its side, clip it to the side of the can, close and turn the handle. Have you ever been cut by an opened can using this "taught method"? Be honest! I know I have. Have you seen the viral video that has made us all question our mothers, grandmothers, and even great grandmothers? NO? Well, I watched it 3xs before I tried it. I placed the can opener flat on top of the can, clipped it, closed, and turned it. The can opened and VOILA - NO SHARP EDGES - NONE?!

What else do you need to unlearn that could potentially make all the difference in how you operate?

2. Level Up

In my time as a #BrandMaster, I've come across designs I easily notice could use enhancements but said nothing. I've watched movies and quickly noticed an error, an inconsistency, a missed event, a misplaced scene or set design, yet I did not receive this as a gift.

Additionally, while attending workshops, events, or otherwise, I immediately recognize missing elements, skipped sequencing areas, or ways the conference flow would better serve attendees. When my colleague and I hosted our own conference, it was praised by the VP of Marketing as one of the best conferences he'd ever attended in the history of the company. He also said he would've never known it was our first. We attribute that to being so well-versed in our notes and a keen eye for detail during the many conferences we'd attended. Our participation in numerous events taught us how to create a duplicate, as well as how to level up and make our events unforgettable.

What do you already know that you could put your spin on and level up to your version of perfection?

3. Become Unbothered

A Chinese Proverb says, "The person who says it cannot be done should not interrupt the person doing it."

It is as easy as walking once you start, and over time, you will become so well versed you could do it blindly. Turning down the volume on all the noise is mandatory to walk out your passion. How can you shift and become unbothered by ANY outside distractions? Make a plan and remain focused on the light at the end of your tunnel.

Once you unlearn the negative, level up, and enhance your gifts, you can stay the course and get to YOUR intended end! Using these steps to release preprogramming is how I've been able to Unleash My Undeniable Impact!

My name is Martina Britt Yelverton, and I am a...

+ BrandMaster
+ CashflowQueen
+ Founder of the #1 Hire Your Kids Legal Tax Hack Movement

Martina Britt Yelverton

I help people who want help! If you need the help I've been blessed to offer, follow me and select the bell for alerts when I go live on YouTube or Facebook!

FREE CONTENT is available at http://youtube.martinabrittyelverton.com.

If you've struggled as a #Parent, as an #Entrepreneur, as a #Brand or #HomeBasedBusiness owner, I can help you:

+ #GetYoASSetsInOrder
+ #GetBranded
+ #GetFound On Google
+ #GetPaid Daily

If you're serious, text "brandmaster" to 474747 TODAY!